S.M.C.

D0340310

Praise for *Thank the Liberals*

"In his lively new book, Alan Colmes makes a very persuasive case that the liberal principles inside all of us—even the most conservative—are to be celebrated, not shunned. **Thank the Liberals** *will make some readers smile and others grit their teeth, but everyone who reads it will have a new appreciation for the way progressive ideals have shaped, and continue to shape, our country."*

— **President Bill Clinton**

"What is liberalism really? And why has it been demonized by some? Alan Colmes wants a kinder, gentler debate, and this book provides an interesting pathway to achieve that."

— **Fox News Anchor Bill O'Reilly**

"In this partisan climate, Alan Colmes achieves something exceptional. In **Thank the Liberals***, he provides an unabashed defense of liberal ideology, while reminding us that at the end of the day we are all Americans."*

— **Congressman Dennis Kucinich**

"I'm pretty sure that if you're a conservative, you didn't buy Alan Colmes' book on purpose! And if you're a liberal, you probably wouldn't be interested in what I would say about it. But Alan is a liberal I like, not because we agree on anything, but because he actually thinks through his viewpoints and can carry on an intense, but grown-up discussion with people whose views he thinks are Neanderthalesque—like mine! Conservatives should read this book to find out what the more intelligent and reasonable element of the 'other side' really believes, and liberals ought to read it because Alan isn't as crazy as the other liberals writing books and it will keep them busy for a while!"

— **Mike Huckabee**

"In **Thank the Liberals***, my good friend Alan Colmes identifies one of the most important, yet frequently overlooked, truths in this country: that we are all connected. In an age dominated by fearful little men who try to keep us apart, it's inspiring to see Alan continue to stand tall on the belief that as a nation, our best ideas and highest notes are always going to be found on our common ground. Isolation*

and separation are making this country sick, and if we are going to cure it, we need voices like Alan's to remind us of what we can accomplish when we work together."

— Russell Simmons

"Alan Colmes has always been a gentleman and a friend, and admirably, always willing to debate ideas rather than lapsing into partisan talking points. As a result, I have always considered him a Liberal rather than just a Democrat. In **Thank the Liberals**, Alan lays out the modern progressive viewpoint in a clear and concise 200 pages. While I disagree with his overall conclusion that the state is a benign force in American life, I also find areas where our opinions overlap. Libertarians and conservatives used to be called 'classical liberals,' and it is vitally important that we have an honest debate with modern liberals. **Thank the Liberals** helps advance that debate."

— Congressman Ron Paul

"I thank Alan Colmes for showing us in his book that the core of our being is already liberal. Irrespective of our political preference, we all seek equality, justice, and freedom. Read this book and affirm your own truth."

— Deepak Chopra

"With one word change, this would be a great book. Just change Liberals to Conservatives."

— Ann Coulter

"Alan Colmes has been on the front lines of progressive values for many years. This book brilliantly captures how an organized and motivated citizenry has pushed our society toward higher and higher levels of justice, tolerance, and peace. And, he eloquently reminds us of our responsibility to carry that torch in order to reduce suffering in our world."

— Congressman Tim Ryan

THANK the LIBERALS

ALSO BY ALAN COLMES

Red, White & Liberal: How Left Is Right & Right Is Wrong

THANK the LIBERALS*

*FOR SAVING AMERICA
(AND WHY YOU SHOULD)

ALAN COLMES

3 1336 09004 9017

HAY HOUSE, INC.
Carlsbad, California • New York City
London • Sydney • Johannesburg
Vancouver • Hong Kong • New Delhi

Copyright © 2012 by Alan Colmes

Published and distributed in the United States by: Hay House, Inc.:
www.hayhouse.com® • *Published and distributed in Australia by:*
Hay House Australia Pty. Ltd.: www.hayhouse.com.au • *Published
and distributed in the United Kingdom by:* Hay House UK, Ltd.:
www.hayhouse.co.uk • *Published and distributed in the Republic
of South Africa by:* Hay House SA (Pty), Ltd.: www.hayhouse.co.za
• *Distributed in Canada by:* Raincoast: www.raincoast.com • *Published in India by:* Hay House Publishers India: www.hayhouse.co.in

Interior design: Riann Bender • *Photo of Alan Colmes:* Brian Marcus-
fredmarcus.com

All rights reserved. No part of this book may be reproduced by
any mechanical, photographic, or electronic process, or in the form of
a phonographic recording; nor may it be stored in a retrieval system,
transmitted, or otherwise be copied for public or private use—other
than for "fair use" as brief quotations embodied in articles and reviews—without prior written permission of the publisher.

"The Case for Liberalism: a defense of the future against the past"
by George S. McGovern (excerpts). Copyright © 2002 by Harper's
Magazine. All rights reserved. Reproduced from the December issue
by special permission.

Library of Congress Cataloging-in-Publication Data

Thank the liberals for saving America (and why you should) / Alan
Colmes. -- 1st ed.
     p. cm.
  Includes bibliographical references.
  ISBN 978-1-4019-4054-6 (hardcover : alk. paper)
  1. Liberalism--United States. I. Colmes, Alan.
JC574.2.U6T53 2012
  320.51'30973--dc23

                                    2012018979

Hardcover ISBN: 978-1-4019-4054-6
Digital ISBN: 978-1-4019-4056-0

15 14 13 12   4 3 2 1
1st edition, August 2012

Printed in the United States of America

CONTENTS

For Jocelyn

INTRODUCTION

A few years ago, on a bored Thanksgiving weekend, on a rare day when I had too much time on my hands, I started blogging. I decided to call my domain "Liberaland," because I believe America is just that—a liberal land where, as the site's tongue-in-cheek logo indicates, all the states are blue, even if some are bluer than others. I didn't know if I'd keep going with the website, but once I began I couldn't stop. For one thing, writing helped solidify my thinking and helped me prepare for my radio show and my television appearances. As I continued to produce material for the site, and as I thought more about this concept, I came to believe that America truly *is* Liberaland. And that's where the idea for this book began.

I firmly believe that almost every American holds many liberal views and that conservatives have many more of them than they'll admit. Sorry if that makes certain heads explode, but this ain't Iran. We live in one of the freest nations on earth, and that, in and of itself, makes you a liberal. If you identify as conservative, just wait . . . I'll show you otherwise. And liberals, you already know you're liberal, but I'll show you why more of us need to be proud of that.

For too long the word *liberal* has languished in a pool of disrepute, demonized by detractors as representing all that's wrong with our country—even though America was founded upon and has progressed along liberal lines, advancing because of liberal efforts. A well-honed right-wing message machine has been in full force for years, grinding out focus-group-tested definitions of what a liberal is, in keeping with the concept of defining the enemy before the enemy can define itself. This effort has successfully turned one of our great American ideals into a dirty word, so much so that many liberals have taken to calling themselves "progressives" to avoid the dreaded "L" word. But, as Americans, we shouldn't shy away from this term: *liberal* and *liberty* both derive from the same root, tracing their origins back to the Latin *liber,* which means *free.* This is one reason why I proudly stand by my claim to being a liberal. In fact, I use the terms *liberal* and *progressive* interchangeably, both in this book and in life, and proudly claim both as calling cards. Conversely, I refer to the other side as *regressives,* and that description needs no further explanation.

The conservative assault on the word *liberal* continues, but it hasn't deterred me from using it in the title of both my previous book and this one. In fact, the besmirching of the word has inspired me to do so. Brilliant wordsmiths like Frank Luntz work with Republicans to define issues in ways that make liberals look bad by default and give conservatives the linguistic edge to sell their views to the American people. Much of Luntz's advice involves making government the enemy and tagging liberals as the proprietors of this evil enterprise. For example, in 2009, a Luntz memo advised Republicans how to fight "the 'Washington takeover' of healthcare." He encouraged use of the words *waste, fraud,* and *abuse* and told conservatives to favor the word *reform,* even though that's exactly what they were fighting against. Frank denied to me, however, that he created the phrase *death panels*. That honor seems to belong to Sarah Palin, or at least to the person who writes reminders on her palm. All of these efforts have left the impression that a liberal is an odd breed that conservatives can't quite understand.

Thank the Liberals will show you that liberal ideals are nothing to be ashamed of; in fact, they're something we all share. You'll see just why the claims of anti-Americanism hurled at liberals are beyond the pale. America was born liberal—the Declaration of Independence puts forth a liberal mission statement, and the Constitution lays out a liberal framework for how the business of our nation is to be conducted. At the time, America was, in fact, *beyond* liberal—it was radical to leave the protection of the motherland and escape from the long arm of the throne and its state-run religion by establishing a new republic, while demanding independence and taxation only with representation.

Contrary to the romantic notion that our founders were hail-fellows-well-met, we had a bunch of renegades who had a groundbreaking idea but were divided by great dissension over how to achieve it. For example, Thomas Jefferson believed in the power of the state and

Alexander Hamilton was a federalist, but while waging intense battles about process, they founded a new nation that survives to this day because of the blueprint they created. We are now living their liberal vision of America.

And as we've moved from our founding to the present day, America has become progressively more liberal. So much of what we take for granted in our daily lives is because of advancements initiated by liberals. Laws passed by liberal legislators often faced great opposition from those on the Right, even as all sides eventually came to see that what was being done was right—er—correct for America. Union activists, so often reviled today, fought for base pay, days off, vacations, and equal pay for women, and sometimes paid for their efforts with their lives. Medicare, Medicaid, Social Security, and so many of the programs that are part of our national DNA exist because of battles waged by liberals.

You will read about many of these hard-fought battles as you work your way through these pages. And you'll see how the Supreme Court has often stepped in to uphold some of our most basic rights, affirming our founders' liberal intentions. These battles aren't just about whether we moved left or right but whether we would glide forward or slide backward. Over time, thankfully, we moved ahead, even if we sometimes had to drag regressives kicking and screaming with us.

And the battle hasn't ended. We continually fight the Right to move America forward. I hope you won't put this book down for some new escape novel or run screaming from your easy chair before you get to the part of the book that speaks to our present conflicts. What are the issues that define us? What is the role of government, and why do liberals believe in it more than conservatives do? Why do we continue to fight for voting rights? Who are the most vulnerable groups among us, and why do they still need protection? And what should our policies be toward the poor, immigrants, gays, drug users, the environment, and war? Why do we put so much importance on religious tolerance and the separation of church and state? If you're a liberal, I suspect you'll feel supported here. For a little boost, at the end of each chapter, I've outlined some key points as reminders of what you've just read—for those special moments when you need to fight the Right. Conservatives, please don't read this. This part of the book is for liberals only. If you're a conservative, perhaps you won't feel that your liberal loved ones and acquaintances (or your humble author, for that matter) are so crazy after all.

By the time you get to the end of the book, I hope you'll see why I believe so strongly that liberals have been, are, and will continue to be on the right side of history. I've always strived to be kind, even when I'm jabbing the Right. I take some good-natured swipes here, but they're only surface cuts. If space aliens invaded us, we'd band together so fast that we'd forget who's left and who's right. I don't expect that we'll all join hands and sing *Kumbaya*, but let's fight as family members, passionate in our beliefs and yet knowing we love each other underneath it all. With that in mind, we're off to a good liberal start.

If you identify as a conservative, please don't forget a key premise of this book: as an American, you're enough of a liberal not to be excluded. In fact, being a conservative American still earns you charter membership in Club Liberal, as "Thank the Liberals" means all of us.

Don't believe me? Take the test below and see where you fall. You'll be surprised. Then sit back, relax, and enjoy the ride.

How Liberal Are You?

- Do you believe that all men and women are created equal?

- Do you relish being able to speak, assemble, and dissent without worry that the government will arrest you?

- Are you thankful for Social Security, Medicare, or Medicaid?

- Do you enjoy having weekends, personal days, and vacations?

- Have you ever loved someone regardless of his or her religious or political beliefs?

- Should an uninsured patient in a coma be treated?

- Are you thankful that the cost of your bananas isn't higher?

- Would you love your child just the same if he or she were gay?

- What if she told you she had had an abortion?

- Have you ever used birth control?

If you answered "yes" to:

- 1–3 of these questions, you have liberal tendencies.

- 3–6 of them, you are definitely a liberal.

- 7 or more, your ACLU card is on the way.

CHAPTER ONE

YOU'RE A LIBERAL

(BUT MAY NOT KNOW IT)

You're a liberal. If you think you're a conservative, this assertion is surely quite shocking. You may even be so upset upon reading this that you're considering either throwing this book down, shooting a hole in it with your shotgun, or, even worse, burning it the way Florida pastor Terry Jones burned the Koran. Or you may feel the need to toss this book aside, even temporarily, and find solace in the Bible. However, that's a fairly liberal book, too, so it may not help you get any more comfortable than this one will. The very fact that you haven't done any of these things (yet) shows how open-minded you are. So don't disappoint and go all Terry Jones on me here.

If right now you're saying, "But Alan, there's no way I'm a liberal," just do me the favor of hearing me out. Exhibit A to prove my point that you're a liberal—maybe in conservative clothing—is that you are an American. (If you're not an American, keep reading; you'll discover how great it is to be one.) As an American, you're free right now to put down this book (don't), go outside for a walk, take a drive, or head for the nearest airport and fly anywhere in the world (except some non-liberal countries). Or, you can stay home, go online, and get almost any information you want without it being firewalled by the government. And that's largely because liberals have stood up against such regulations as the Stop Online Piracy Act (SOPA) and the Protect IP Act (PIPA) that would have squelched free speech on the Internet and made criminals out of innocent content creators. This doesn't mean the government hasn't already overreached. Even if the government knows what websites you're going to because of the very unpatriotic Patriot Act, they're likely not paying too much attention to you and won't do anything about it. You want to leave your job, start a business, go to a food court and gorge out, or just goof off—this is the land of the free, so go ahead (after you're done with this book).

The United States Constitution has proved itself the most marvelously elastic compilation of rules of government ever written. *~Franklin D. Roosevelt*

America was founded on a liberal idea. The concept of a representative democracy without a state religion was a move leftward from the motherland, where the Church of England dictated certain laws and mores.

Our forefathers thought that a state religion was repressive, and so they established one of our key tenets: freedom of (and from) religion. There can be no religious test to hold public office in America. That's liberal. A commander-in-chief who's a civilian, not a member of the military: liberal. Taxation with representation: liberal. A tripartite form of government where no branch can rule the other: yep, that's liberal, too.

Our founders, the ones conservatives revere so much, took these very liberal ideas and made them so much a part of our DNA that America is unthinkable without them.

Let's look at some of the parts of our founding document that don't often get enough press but show how liberal we are simply because we're American.

Article I, Section 8 lays out the rights of Congress, stating in part that they have the right to "lay and collect Taxes, Duties, Imposts, and Excises, to pay the Debts and provide for the common Defence and general Welfare of the United States." That the government is specifically charged with providing for the "general Welfare" of our population has been much disputed by conservatives. Over time, liberals have fought for numerous items that fall in this category that have greatly benefited Americans, programs conservatives forget they initially opposed. You'll read about them later, in the chapter "Have You Thanked a Liberal Today?"

Article I, Section 8 also guarantees your right to your personal intellectual property by saying that Congress has the right to "promote the Progress of Science and useful Arts, by securing for limited Times to Authors and Inventors the exclusive Right to their respective Writings and Discoveries." If you invent something or write something, it's not the property of the government. This is why entrepreneurs and scientists flock to America. They know that here they are free to create and that they will get the credit they deserve for their work.

Our founding document establishes our court system, giving us a way to seek redress for grievances. The Constitution establishes the creation of various courts, available for different purposes, depending on the issue at hand. Congress has the authority to create bankruptcy courts and tax courts to handle specific issues. Article III says, "The judicial Power of the United States, shall be vested in one supreme Court, and in such inferior Courts as the Congress may from time to time ordain and establish," giving us a federal court system and an appeals process.

Article I, Section 9 gives us the right to seek relief from unlawful imprisonment. A prisoner or someone on his or her behalf can petition for a "writ" of habeas corpus—an order from the government that it has the right to detain the person in question. This protects us from being held arbitrarily by the state, without evidence or just cause.

Our entire judicial system, outlined in the Bill of Rights—the first ten amendments of our Constitution— is built upon a liberal idea. The focus is on protecting the individual, especially the minority, from the tyranny of the majority. For example, the presumption of innocence, which is implied by the right to remain silent and the right to a jury, places the burden of proof on the prosecutor.

The Fifth Amendment calls for grand juries to protect us from being prosecuted when there isn't enough evidence to bring a case against us. This amendment also guarantees that we can't be tried for the same crime twice and that we are protected from having to testify against ourselves. This was originally written to guard against torture and forced confession. Most important, we can't be deprived of life, liberty, or property without "due process of law." If charged with a crime, there is a process in place to guarantee us a fair trial. This includes being given adequate notice to prepare a defense against those charges. The Fifth Amendment also contains the promise that the government can't take our property away without just compensation. We probably take all of this for granted, but that's probably because we've never lived in a country where a terrifying knock on the door at 3 A.M. could mean a phony trial in a kangaroo court or a demand that we leave our homes because someone from the government needs or wants them.

The Sixth Amendment continues the discussion of our judicial system through the promise that anyone accused of committing a crime has the right to a speedy and public trial by an impartial jury of peers, in the jurisdiction where the alleged crime was committed. You have the right to be told the charges against you, to confront your accuser in court, to have witnesses on your behalf, and to have counsel represent you. And if you can't afford a lawyer, the state will provide one. These guarantees, so particular to our way of life, arose from the liberal thinking of our forebears.

In the Seventh Amendment, we are guaranteed the right to a jury trial in civil cases, such as resolving disputes between individuals and organizations. This amendment also tells us that when a jury in one court makes a factual determination, it can't be overturned by another court.

Our Eighth Amendment says the punishment has to fit the crime: there can be no excessive fines or sentences like having your arm cut off for stealing a loaf of bread. Certain kinds of punishment are specifically outlawed, no matter how heinous the crime—that's where the "no cruel and unusual punishment" clause comes in. In America, you can't be hanged, drawn, and quartered (dragged by a horse to your hanging, then cut into four pieces). You can't be burned alive or dissected or disemboweled. Even though an unruly mob may wish it on a despicable criminal, our Constitution guarantees that no person is ever treated with this kind of cruelty. Also, we don't execute the mentally handicapped or those under age 18.

Due process is also called for in the Fourteenth Amendment, which takes the protection of life, liberty, and property guaranteed in the Fifth Amendment and expands it to apply to state and local governments as well. The Fourteenth Amendment also contains the Equal Protection Clause, which extends the same guarantees to everyone, regardless of race, creed, color, or religion. It arose out of the ending of slavery and the overturning of *Dred Scott v. Sandford,* which ruled that blacks could not be citizens of the United States. With Amendment Fourteen, anyone born or naturalized in the United States is a citizen, and Americans have representation in Congress based on our true population—a population that includes *all* citizens, not just white men. A number of other liberal ideas laid out in our Constitution help set us apart from other countries. We are not subject to the whims of a dictator who could decide we are acting against the best interests of the country. That is why, in Article III of the Constitution, treason is specifically defined to mean declaring war on our country or giving aid and comfort to an enemy. In America, it's not treasonous to disagree with the powers that be, a protection further enhanced by our First Amendment.

Americans are also protected through specific regulations on our government. Our presidents are term-limited, and they have to report the "State of the Union" to Congress every year. Plus, there is a process to throw the bum out if he (or she) commits a high crime or misdemeanor. But let's not forget that presidents are Americans, too, and they need protection against unjust acts. So, even if a president is impeached, which is simply an accusation, it takes a two-thirds majority of the Senate to convict. This purposely high bar—the ruling supermajority—is required for conviction, to avoid a partisan witch hunt. It couldn't even be reached when a highly politicized Republican Senate voted on whether Bill Clinton should be thrown out of office for lying about a sexual relationship. Our liberal Constitution protects not only private citizens but also elected ones from being unfairly treated. When you celebrate our freedom, it's because of these very liberal considerations that our founders codified. And there's much more.

In addition to the judicial guarantees already discussed, the Bill of Rights establishes our personal freedoms. Empowering the individual over the government was a progressive concept when it was implemented and remains one today. Our First Amendment, which guarantees freedom of speech and assembly, takes religion out of the state's purview, and further promises a way to redress grievances, is a shining example of what a liberal country stands for, and it has withstood the test of time. Even the right to bear arms is a liberal concept, though some people have gone a bit crazy with it and forgotten that no right is absolute.

Among other liberties guaranteed in the Bill of Rights: A soldier can't barge into your house and demand shelter. That's a pretty good one that doesn't get mentioned very often, and it's our Third Amendment. The Fourth Amendment guarantees that you are secure in your home, that the government can't randomly check what's in your dresser without a warrant. If someone in a government uniform wants to know what you're up to, you don't have to tell him or her, or let the person into your home without a court order. I have so often heard from conservatives arguments like, "If I've done nothing wrong, I've got nothing to worry about." The better response is, "If I've done nothing wrong, the government has nothing to worry about." If you are okay welcoming uniformed agents into your home at any time, without your consent, you would have been very comfortable living under rulers like Josef Stalin or Saddam Hussein.

One of the wonderful promises our founders made to us is that our rights don't necessarily begin and end with those listed in the Constitution. Thus, the Ninth Amendment says, "The enumeration in the Constitution, of certain rights, shall not be construed to deny or disparage others retained by the people." Just in case something comes up that isn't specified, we are protected. Our founders were prescient enough to know that not everything could be covered in a relatively short document. They also knew that not everything they wrote would hold for eternity.

Nevertheless, our nation's blueprint was so well devised that it's been altered only a handful of times. And almost every time it was amended, it liberalized our country even more. The Thirteenth Amendment, for example, ended slavery and involuntary servitude, and the Fourteenth Amendment, as mentioned before, made sure that former slaves were recognized as American citizens with all the rights that go along with that. The Fourteenth Amendment has also been cited to make sure that blacks are not kept off juries, to provide equal education for blacks and whites, and to apportion congressional districts to ensure "one man, one vote." Amendment Fifteen ensured that former slaves could vote, and that going forward, neither color nor previous servitude would be an impediment to voting.

The Seventeenth Amendment, adopted in 1913, put more power in the hands of Americans by giving them the power to vote for United States senators. Until then, state legislatures chose the senators. Vesting that privilege in the general population gave us more say about who represents us. The Nineteenth Amendment gave women the vote, further empowering the citizenry. More voting enfranchisement came with the Twenty-fourth Amendment, which did away with the poll tax. Until then, poorer Americans were prevented from voting if they couldn't afford to pay up. Voting rights were expanded again with the Twenty-sixth Amendment, which lowered the minimum voting age from 21 to 18. It was finally determined that those who are asked to serve in the armed forces and die for our country should have a say in who runs it. The Twenty-first Amendment repealed Prohibition, overturning the wrongheaded Eighteenth, which banned the manufacture, sale, and transport of liquor.

See how progressive our Constitution is?

Contrary to what many conservatives would have you believe, our Constitution is not based on the Bible, but rather on English common law dating back to the 1215

Magna Carta. "Common law" means it arose organically from the people rather than being handed down from some higher authority. Pennsylvania's founder, William Penn, had published a copy of the Magna Carta, and the founders of our colonies used rights enshrined in it to organize our first governments. Much of our Constitution comes directly from the Magna Carta, including the right to a speedy trial, the right to due process, and habeas corpus. But we created even more freedoms than our English forebears. Our legal blueprint goes beyond English common law to establish rights that are uniquely American, making us among the most liberal nations on earth. While the Magna Carta gave people rights to protect them from a monarchy, we retained the rights but made sure there was no monarchy. Article I, Section 9 of our Constitution says there shall be "no Title of Nobility," which means that we don't have power centralized in any one, unelected person. "No Title of Nobility" means we don't have kings and queens in America. Well, Ralph Kramden was the king of his castle, and Aretha is the Queen of Soul, but that's because of wonderful comedy and musical acts, not congressional ones. If you want an honorific other than *Mr.*, *Mrs.*, or *Ms.* in America, you have to earn it at an institution of higher learning.

Without Thomas Jefferson and his Declaration of Independence, there would have been no American revolution that announced universal principles of liberty. *~Christopher Hitchens*

English common law didn't go far enough for a people that was more progressive, and that shows in another of our founding documents, the very liberal Declaration of Independence. Here we are guaranteed not just legal rights but also natural rights—rights beyond what any culture or government can give us. The Declaration was our notice of separation from an empire that didn't grant us the freedoms we cherish. It declares that "all men are created equal" and have the "unalienable" right to "Life, Liberty, and the pursuit of Happiness." Key to the thinking that gave us these words is that these rights aren't something granted to us by some noble class or even by our officials. They are "endowed" by a "Creator," whatever you perceive that creator to be. If you aren't a God-believer, you can chalk it up to "Laws of Nature," another way our founders put it in the Declaration. The opening paragraph calls for "a decent respect to the opinions of mankind"—we wanted England to respect our choices, and we need to respect those of other sovereign nations. This is something good to remember when we are critical of other, non-American ways of life.

The Declaration also asserts that for our "Safety and Happiness," we have the right to "alter or to abolish" a government "whenever . . . [it] becomes destructive." To this end, the document lists grievances against the King of England, who would not "assent to laws . . . for the public good" and who repeatedly dissolved the legislature when it didn't meet his needs, without holding elections to replace it. Judges were dependent on the king for their salaries and length of service, and so there was no true balance of power. And there was taxation without the consent of the governed, which came to a head when Britain forced the colonies to do business with the East India Tea Company and pay taxes on the tea over which the colonies had no control. This became the basis of the Boston Tea Party: the colonists decided just to get rid of all that tea being shipped over to them by throwing it into the harbor. This was the *real* Tea Party, not the ersatz one created by disgruntled conservatives in the 21st century who already *had* representation.

Laid out in our separation statement from our mother country was not a request but a declaration, an assertion that man is, by nature, free and that no person, no king, no government can ever change that. We made a pledge to each other, as fellow countrymen, to uphold our unalienable rights to protect "our Lives, our Fortunes, and our sacred Honor." That word *unalienable*—in modern usage, *inalienable*—refers to what cannot be taken away. As human beings, we deserve respect simply because we exist and are imbued with dignity that cannot be destroyed by anything outside of us—no person, no government, no entity of any kind. The word *inalienable* gets tossed around a lot, but it gets at the heart of true freedom. It is what truly sets America apart as a more progressive land than had previously existed. It is why, to this day, immigrants flock here to drink from our fountain of freedom and to breathe in our American molecules. If we're born here, we're so immersed in this concept, practically from birth, that we don't know any other way. That is why those who come here from repressive regimes often have a greater appreciation of what freedom truly means than we do. Try telling someone who escaped from Saddam Hussein's Iraq or the Soviet gulags that America isn't a very liberal place to be.

If you proudly wave the conservative banner, you're not as conservative as you think. You'd stand up and fight against anything that would take away our enumerated rights. You wave around the Constitution as a revered work that must be honored. You quote the Declaration of Independence when challenged on patriotism. Thus, you are a defender of the very liberal notions laid out in these documents. Would you stand for anyone taking away your freedom to speak, to assemble, to have a fair trial, or to practice your religion? Of course not—you'd defend to the death these liberal precepts.

I'm a conservative, but I'm not a nut about it.
~*George H. W. Bush*

Okay. So we've seen that you're a liberal just because you're an American. Now let's move to Exhibit B in my effort to convince you of your liberal leanings: your day-to-day life. You may be a passionate believer in certain conservative ideas and policies, but would you spring into action with them when opportunities arose? I say, not necessarily. Professed attitudes toward abortion, gay rights, immigration, and many other hot-button issues don't comport with the way we actually live.

You may be vehemently opposed to illegal immigrants residing in our country. But you're probably happy to munch on the fruit they pick for you or to have your lawn beautifully manicured by someone whose papers may not be in order. There's a good chance that people whose services you use every day are not legal residents, and you don't even know it. The driver who takes you to the hospital, the nurse who attends to you, the waiter who brings you your dinner, or the ball player you root for may have, for all you know, sneaked into the country in the dead of night. Do you want to be the one to knock on their doors, break them away from their families, escort them to the border, and push them back to where they came from? The difference between what ideologues tell us to do and how we actually live our lives stood out in bas-relief during an October 2011 presidential debate where immigration policy was a hot topic. Texas Governor Rick Perry criticized fellow candidate Mitt Romney for having once used a landscaping service that employed undocumented workers. If you've ever had work done on your home, there's a good chance that a subcontractor or two may not have been a legal resident of the United States, but did you go around asking to see the papers of everyone trimming your hedges or plastering your walls? Probably not. But Mitt Romney claimed otherwise: "We went to the company and we said, 'Look, you can't have any illegals working on our property. I'm running for office, for Pete's sake. I can't have illegals.'" See, it wasn't so much that Romney objected to having undocumented workers on his property. That's par for the course in America. If his tale is true, his desire to remove such interlopers from his property had nothing to do with real life and everything to do with the potential fallout in a political campaign.

Abortion is another area where personal experience can trump tightly held beliefs. It's been legal in the United States since 1973 and has remained so in spite of conservative presidents and legislatures vowing to end a woman's right to enjoy reproductive freedom.

Even top Republicans find themselves leaning toward a more liberal stance on the issue of abortion when it comes to their personal lives. In 1992, when Dan Quayle was running for vice president on the Republican ticket with George W. Bush, Larry King asked Quayle how he'd react if his daughter were pregnant. "Well, it is a hypothetical situation, and I hope that I never do have to deal with it," was the immediate answer. Then: "I would counsel her and talk to her and support her on whatever decision she made." This created a mini-firestorm on the campaign trail and an "aha!" moment, with the realization that Mr. Quayle's response was the most humane answer he could have provided. He answered as a loving father, not as a politician looking to raise money from a special interest group.

Even when it doesn't affect their personal lives, many ambitious pols are pro-choice by default but move to an anti-choice position when politics demand it. Gerald Ford wasn't an anti-abortion politician, but he had to support the Human Life Amendment (which would repeal *Roe v. Wade*) if he wanted to get the 1976 presidential nomination. George H. W. Bush was pro-choice when he sought his party's nod in 1980, but amazingly (or maybe not so surprisingly), he became anti-choice by the time he finished up as Ronald Reagan's vice president and got the nod in 1988.

You don't have to dig deep before you discover the power of political appearances on this issue. Mitt Romney's stance on abortion has been historically liberal, even after his "epiphany," when he claimed to have had an instantaneous reversal of his previous pro-choice position after meeting with a Harvard University stem cell researcher in November 2004. This is the man who, in 1994, publicly supported women having access to the abortion pill RU-486, stating, "I think it would be a positive thing to have women have the choice of taking the morning-after pill. . . . I would favor having it available." In his 2002 race for governor of Massachusetts Romney told an interviewer, "So when asked, 'Will I preserve and protect a woman's right to choose?' I make an unequivocal answer: yes." But when, in a 2004, the

Harvard scientist told him embryos were "killed" after 14 days, Romney proclaimed, "It hit me very hard, that we had so cheapened the value of human life in a *Roe v. Wade* environment that it was important to stand for the dignity of human life." Epiphany notwithstanding, Romney continued to govern as a pro-choicer, appointing pro-choice judge Matthew Nestor to a district court, for one thing. And in December 2005, Romney ordered his administration to require Catholic hospitals to provide emergency contraception to rape victims. Some epiphany! But then on the 39th anniversary of *Roe v. Wade* in January 2012—right after losing a brutal South Carolina primary to Newt Gingrich—Romney issued a news release calling the *Roe v. Wade* decision "one of the darkest moments in Supreme Court history." This was a complete about-face from his signed response to a Planned Parenthood questionnaire in 2002 in which he said he supported the substance of *Roe v. Wade* as well as "state funding of abortion services through Medicaid for low-income women." In other words, Mitt Romney is no hardcore anti-choicer but believes he has to come off as one for political expediency.

Another 2012 candidate was pro-choice in his heart, even though he couldn't admit it, maybe not even to himself. Herman Cain twisted himself into a pretzel on the abortion issue during his ill-fated presidential campaign. He was going around referring to Planned Parenthood as "planned genocide" and saying the organization's mission was to "help kill black babies before they came into the world." That's a twofer: he got to rail against baby killers *and* play the race card at the same time. But when Piers Morgan asked Cain what he'd do if it were personalized, Cain suddenly no longer sounded like a conservative.

Morgan: Are you honestly saying—again, tricky question I know, but you've had children, grandchildren—if one of your female children, grandchildren was raped, you would honestly want her to bring up that baby as her own?

Cain: You're mixing two things here, Piers . . .

Morgan: Why? . . . that's what it comes down to.

Cain: No, [what] it comes down to [is] it's not the government's role—or anybody else's role—to make that decision. Secondly, if you look at the statistical incidents, you're not talking about that big a number. So what I'm saying is, it ultimately gets down to a choice that that family or that mother has to make. Not me as president. Not some politician. Not a bureaucrat. It gets down to that family. And whatever they decide, they decide. I shouldn't try to tell them what decision to make for such a sensitive decision.

In subsequent interviews, Cain complained that his words were taken out of context, that the media didn't fully present his answer, and that he was only talking about a rare, hypothetical situation. Sorry, but the context is there, it's not the fault of the messenger, and that hypothetical situation happens every day in America.

In an unguarded moment, Herman Cain expressed what Americans inherently know. Nobody is going to tell you what to decide when private, sensitive decisions have to be made. Nobody is going to tell you what religion to be, where to pray, or that you have to pray at all. In spite of some paranoids who think the right to be a Christian in America is being compromised, no one in America is prevented from practicing the religion of his or her choice, or from believing that religion is hogwash. If you want to make a sanctuary in your home, burn incense, and pray to a lamp, no one is going to stop you. If you can find others to share your lamp-as-deity belief, you can rent a hall and all pray together to the fixture of your choice, and you won't be prosecuted. Made fun of, maybe, but even the men and women with the white coats will likely leave you alone if you're not a menace to other people.

Another subject that presents a conservative face on campaign trails, at fundraisers, and on conservative talk shows—but again plays differently in people's personal and professional lives—is the gay issue. Some of the most anti-gay public activists have gay children, and most of them love and support their children, regardless of what they say publically about this lifestyle. Eagle Forum founder Phyllis Schlafly once said of gays wanting equal rights, "The problem is they are trying to make us respect them, and that's an interference with what we believe." And yet, it's likely Schlafly respects her gay son. Asked about him by *Time* magazine in 2009 she said, "Well, I don't try to run my children's lives, and he has been very supportive. He works for Eagle Forum. He runs my operations office, and he's very supportive of all the positions that I've taken." She said he even supports her position against gay marriage. The bottom line, though, is that she loves, supports, and accepts him, in spite of her many public statements against gays.

Dick Cheney is another high-profile figure who, one would think, would stake out anti-gay positions, based on party affiliation, on being George W. Bush's vice president, and on his often-stated commitment to "conservative values." However, likely based on personal experience, he has supported the repeal of the military's anti-gay "Don't Ask, Don't Tell" policy and has spoken in favor of gay marriage. His gay daughter, Mary, has done much to help the former vice president evolve his own thinking on equality. She recounts her father's reaction to her coming out in her book *Now It's My Turn:* "You're my daughter, and I love you and I just want you to be happy." Can you imagine any parent having a better reaction?

The gay and abortion topics are wedge issues that right-wing groups use to raise money by telling their followers that if liberals are elected they'll continue to kill babies in the womb and that gays will get special rights that will end up ruining American families. Let's be honest: unnecessary wars have killed too many who've already left the womb, and Kim Kardashian has done more to disrespect the institution of marriage than any gay couple I know. Various polls over the years have shown that the country is divided on these issues, with either side occasionally winning out over the other. But ask someone you know what he or she would do if a daughter got pregnant and wanted to have an abortion, or if a son came home with his friend Ralph to announce they're in love. After the initial shock, and perhaps much soul searching, most parents would support a child in either circumstance.

And why is this? It's because actual life experience can take us out of our preconceived, conservative notions. Discovering that a beloved child is gay or will have an abortion is enough to shock a parent out of a formerly intransigent position. Life experience is why people often get more liberal with age. You've done more things, visited more places, and met more people, and you realize the world isn't the little square box with nicely tied ribbons you believed it to be. Talk to your grandparents. Ask them how much they've stuck to the positions they believed when they were young. You'll be surprised at how, when osmosis meets evolution, the result is organic change.

In fact, science has looked at the myth that people get more conservative as they age, and found it to be just that: a myth. In a 2007 study tracking 46,510 Americans from 1972 to 2004, sociologists Nicholas Danigelis and Stephen Cutler at the University of Vermont and Melissa Hardy at Penn State discovered that people generally get more liberal as they age. Attitudes on race, gender, religion, sexuality, and economics veer leftward with older groups. Portraying older people as cranky and stuck in their ways is nothing more than a stereotype.

Sometimes a change in thinking that comes via life's unexpected moments can happen in the blink of an eye; a traumatic experience that underscores the fragility of life can have a similarly radical effect on your point of view. George Wallace, the bigoted Alabama governor, once vowed, "Segregation today . . . segregation tomorrow . . . segregation forever." In June 1963 he stood in a doorway at the University of Alabama to stop integrated enrollment. This became known as "The Stand in the Schoolhouse Door." But after intervention by the federal government, the governor had to stand down. That fall, he again tried to get in the way of black students at four Huntsville elementary schools, but again he had to step aside when ordered by a court, allowing the first primary and secondary schools to be integrated in Alabama.

Wallace's life changed in 1972 while campaigning for the Democratic nomination for president in Laurel, Maryland. He was shot five times by Arthur Bremer, an unstable man seeking infamy. A bullet lodged in his spinal column, paralyzing him and causing him pain for the rest of his life. Wallace's presidential ambitions were destroyed, and the trauma blunted more than just his physical abilities. It deeply impacted his most ardent beliefs.

While many remember Wallace as a segregationist and a bigot, he rarely gets credit for his change of heart. In 1979, making an unannounced appearance at the Dexter Avenue Baptist Church, a black congregation in Montgomery whose pastor was once Martin Luther King, Jr., Wallace explained being a changed man: "I have learned what suffering means. In a way that was impossible before [the shooting], I think I can understand something of the pain black people have come to endure. I know I contributed to that pain, and I can only ask your forgiveness."

During his last term as governor in the mid-1980s, Wallace had a black press secretary and hired 160 black appointees. He doubled the number of black registrars in Alabama's 67 counties. By the end of his life, as recounted in Stephan Lesher's biography, *George Wallace: American Populist*, Wallace was praying with Jesse Jackson and joining hands in black churches and singing "We Shall Overcome." Lesher described Wallace as having "a humanity so often lacking in his actions: alone and crippled, forced to introspection for the first time in his life, he realized that though he had purported to be the champion of the poor and the helpless, he had

trampled on the poorest and most helpless of all his con-
stituents—the blacks."

So you see, some of our most ardent conservatives
had and have some very liberal ways about them. Text-
book positions often don't fit in with the way we live
our lives, and often as we experience more, we change
these opinions. When faced with real life, most people
do the human thing. That's so much a part of being an
American.

**America is a liberal idea . . . It's hard to be an American
conservative because that's a contradiction in terms.**
~Jesse Jackson

We created our nation based on liberal ideas, and
these notions are bred into us from the moment we take
our first breaths. If you are lucky enough to be born and
grow up in America you know instinctively that freedom
is yours simply for being alive. And our founding documents make that official. They tell us that our right to
be happy, to pursue our dreams, to have liberty, are such
a part of the human condition that no government can
give them to you. It's automatic. Because if it weren't,
the government would be able to take them away. That
is not possible in America.

Our Declaration of Independence is a beautiful mission statement that along with our finely crafted Constitution, established America as a liberal beacon that
would shine a light on the rest of the world. We continue
to present ourselves as a force for good on the planet. We
may not always live up to these ideals, but to our credit,
we believe these ideals are worth striving for. It's inspiring to be reminded about the intent of our founders,

perfect in their imperfections, and about the good will and kindheartedness we have as Americans.

As former South Dakota senator and 1972 Democratic presidential nominee George McGovern wrote in "The Case for Liberalism: A Defense of the Future against the Past" for the December 2002 issue of *Harper's*:

> Except for the most confirmed standpatter or unswerving cynic, nearly all Americans have some identification with liberalism, whether they know it or not. Just about every educated person I encounter around the world is a liberal. Almost every working journalist, nurse, and flight attendant leans toward liberalism; nearly every teacher, scientist, clergyman, and child-care worker is a liberal. I can't remember the last time I met an illiberal professor of history, my old profession. How could anybody read history and not be a liberal?

Should despotism ever rear its head, it is not just our right, but our duty to change course. Surely, no reasonable citizen in the land of liberty could disagree.

A LITTLE HELP TO FIGHT THE RIGHT

All Americans are liberals; *American conservative* is an oxymoron.

America was founded on liberal ideas, as outlined in the liberal Bill of Rights and Declaration of Independence.

A religion-free, representative government, checks and balances, a civilian-run military, and no concentration of power in nobility are liberal ideas that separate the United States from the motherland.

The Constitution isn't based on the Bible, but rather on English Common Law, which we expanded upon because it didn't go far enough for the liberal founders of America.

Conservatives' views often don't comport with their personal actions.

Those who rail against homosexuality and abortion tend to have different views when they face these issues in their personal lives.

Anti-immigration proponents aren't strict in checking papers of all those who perform services in their lives.

Actual life experience changes the way you look at life; both age and life's dramas can shift views.

American and *Liberal* are practically synonyms.

CHAPTER TWO

HAVE YOU THANKED A LIBERAL TODAY?

If you are a conservative reading this, I may not have yet helped you get in touch with your inner liberal, in which case I may have more success on that score in this chapter. After all, many of the freedoms we enjoy today are because of what liberals have fought to accomplish.

Try taking away Medicare, Medicaid, or Social Security and see how that goes down. Politicians like Congressman Paul Ryan and his Republican brethren can try to reduce these staples at their own political peril. It's also because of liberals that we have protected bank deposits, a minimum wage, weekends and vacations, civil rights, Pell education grants, a government net for the needy, equal pay for equal work, birth control availability, the Family and Medical Leave Act, and well, I'm about to run out of commas. In the next chapter,

"Progress Affirmed!," I'll show how these policies held up under Supreme Court scrutiny, further cementing our liberal heritage. More often than not the Court has stood up for what's right by affirming policies initiated by the Left.

If you didn't already know it, you can see by what I wrote in the last chapter that George McGovern is an unrepentant liberal. He may not have won the presidency, but he has stood up for the kind of values Republicans claim to promote and for the kind of progress that liberals have historically offered. Frankly, we might be in much better shape today had the decorated former WWII B-24 fighter pilot won in 1972. Here is what he wrote about the accomplishments of liberalism in his *Harper's* article:

> Virtually every step forward in our history has been a liberal initiative taken over conservative opposition: civil rights, Social Security, Medicare, rural electrification, the establishment of a minimum wage, collective bargaining, the Pure Food and Drug Act, and federal aid to education, including the land-grant colleges, to name just a few. Many of these innovations were eventually embraced by conservatives only after it became clear that they had overwhelming public approval for the simple reason that almost every American benefited from them. Every one of these liberal efforts strengthened our democracy and our quality of life.

McGovern added to the list of liberal accomplishments "guaranteed bank deposits, the Federal Reserve, the Securities and Exchange Commission, the Food and Drug Administration, the National Park Service, the

National School Lunch Program, the Voting Rights Act, and the graduated income tax."

I don't expect that everyone agrees on the precise value of each of these plans, but most Americans, liberal or not, must believe that they have made—and continue to make—our life better. Conservatives, it can be shown time and time again, have been on the wrong side of history. Even where Democrats and Republicans have worked together, such as on the Americans with Disabilities Act signed by George H. W. Bush in 1990, conservative religious and business groups objected because they didn't want to spend the money to make their places more accessible to those who needed it. In addition to access to public transportation and places of public accommodation, the ADA is a civil rights measure that ensures equal access to jobs, job training, and other privileges of employment for qualified individuals with disabilities. Thankfully, political will overcame the opposition of those who cared more about the bottom line than equality for all Americans.

What liberals have done, beginning with our founders, is fight for a society of equality and fair play. This goes to the heart of so many of the battles between left and right, particularly as pertains to health care. Given how prominently this figures into our current divisions, let's start right there.

This is a big F***ing Deal ~*Joe Biden*

Taking on the health-care establishment is a big deal, and no modifier in that sentence, not even the one Vice President Joe Biden used, can really do it justice. The Patient Protection and Affordable Care Act is the actual name of the legislation, although its opponents derisively called it "ObamaCare." It was smart of the White House to turn that around during the 2012 campaign when, instead of running away from that snarky name, it decided to embrace it by saying, "Right, Obama *does* care." Because of this advancement, 2.5 million young adults between 19 and 25 years old gained coverage. Insurance companies are now required to spend at least 80 percent of premiums on caring for people, not on salaries or overhead. How many times have you had to call and call again to get a code right on a request for submitted benefits? Insurance companies, until now, have thrived on saying no. That's their job. Well, they're now barred from denying coverage because of a mistake on a form, and when an insurance company says no to a claim, there is now an external review process. Lifetime limits on insurance coverage are lifted. Free preventive care is available for seniors. States are eligible for matching funds to cover poor families not already covered under Medicaid. One of the great early benefits of the new law was to stop discriminating against children who were denied heath care because of preexisting conditions. And those are just the improvements that kicked in at the beginning of 2010 that most people don't even know about. The following year brought annual wellness visits and prescription drug discounts for seniors. As of 2012 hospitals, encouraged by financial incentives, were required to be more accountable for outcomes, and a process was put in place to reduce paperwork and incorporate standard electronic billing. By 2014, adults won't be denied coverage for preexisting conditions or charged more because of gender, and all dollar limits on how much coverage you can receive will be eliminated.

Some of the myths put forward by opponents of this landmark legislation never came to pass. We heard that the act would provide health care for illegal immigrants, that taxpayers would be paying for abortions, that Americans would be forced out of plans they liked, and that there'd be health-care rationing. And let's not forget the ever-popular death panels that were supposed to encourage the elderly to choose early deaths. All untrue.

Interestingly, during the health-care debate we heard reports about poll after poll that told us what percentage of Americans didn't support ObamaCare. What was left out of almost every one of these surveys was how many opposed it from the Left. Ipsos/McClatchy did a poll in November 2009 and discovered that of those who were against the Affordable Care Act, 25 percent didn't think it went far enough. This represented 12 percent of participants in the entire survey. So when conservatives tout percentages of those who don't like the health-care reforms, what you are not hearing is that a significant number of its detractors wish we had a more progressive system in place.

It's the progressives who have historically advocated for health-care reforms, and they have been consistently opposed along the way. Teddy Roosevelt fought for health-insurance reform when he ran as the Progressive Party candidate for President in 1912. The party's platform called for "the protection of home life against the hazards of sickness, irregular employment, and old age, through the adoption of a system of social insurance adapted to American use." Employers would be required to share in the cost of health insurance, and a national health service would be created. However, insurance companies, doctors, businesses, and conservative legislators were vehemently opposed to this, even characterizing it as a Bolshevik plot to take over America. Sound familiar? But Roosevelt and his progressive Bull Moose Party lost the 1912 election.

Where Teddy left off, his fifth cousin, Franklin Delano Roosevelt, stepped in. During his presidency, FDR advocated for health-care reform, and he tried to include health insurance as part of the 1935 Social Security Bill. But because the American Medical Association and conservatives opposed it, it was removed so Social Security could pass. The National Health Act of 1939 would have created a national health program funded by federal grants to the states, but the 1938 election added more conservatives to Congress, and progress couldn't be made. In 1943, Senators Robert Wagner of New York, John Murray of Montana, and John Dingell of Michigan sponsored the Wagner-Murray-Dingell Bill, which would have provided cradle-to-grave health coverage. Mandatory health care would have been paid for by payroll taxes. This bill arose out of the Social Security Charter Committee, but because one of the members of the committee, I. S. Falk, was associated with the International Labor Union, the bill was characterized as part of a "Red" plot.

When Democrat Harry Truman became president, he supported a single, universal health insurance plan, but as the Cold War intensified, the new president's strong support for national health care was linked by its opponents to Communism. Ohio Senator Robert Taft called it "socialism," and rumors spread that the plan was based on the Soviet Constitution. It's amusing to compare how similar the slurs against progressives back then were to what liberals experience today.

Even though Truman had to fight the red-baiters and couldn't get as progressive a health-care plan as he wanted, he was successful in signing the National Mental Health Act, which, for the first time, recognized mental illness as a real issue. This was because returning soldiers from World War II had mental-health issues that, it was discovered, existed prior to their military service. Thus, the level of mental illness in the general population was finally recognized. Now, for the first time, there would be funding for education and research about mental-health issues. Truman also signed the Hill-Burton Act, which made sure that hospitals were up to par and that there were at least 4.5 beds for every 1,000 people in the population. Furthermore, facilities receiving money couldn't discriminate based on race, color, national origin, or creed.

Two paragraphs ago, I wrote how "amusing" it is to see some of the same objections to health-care reform today that we saw back then. Let me modify that. It would be amusing if it weren't so sad. You'd think that with the Cold War over, we'd stop calling our political adversaries "Communists." What do political enemies call each other in the Eastern bloc—"Americans"? Some of the funniest signs at Tea Party rallies during the Obama administration were the ones that said variants of "Keep the government out of health care, and don't touch my Medicare." (My other favorite was "Get a brain morans.") You have to wonder if those people, oblivious to history, would have opposed what Lyndon Baines Johnson did. LBJ's Medicare program provided health care to Americans over age 65, to the permanently disabled, and to those born with disabilities. President Johnson honored Harry Truman by giving him the first Medicare card, and the second one went to Truman's wife, Bess. LBJ also created Medicaid, which provided health care to welfare recipients. Because of Medicaid, infant mortality rates dropped a third between 1965 and 1975. It is difficult to imagine these programs being created in today's environment, and yet they should have been—and should be—a model for providing health care to all.

In fact, Michigan Congressman John Conyers proposed what could be the answer to our health-care dilemma—the United States National Health Care Act, or H.R. 636. It provides that all medically necessary care will be paid for by the government, relegating private insurance to nonessential services. This is not government-run health care but rather government-insured health care. Economist Paul Krugman estimates that the lower administrative costs of this kind of program would save $200 billion a year, enough to cover those currently uninsured and then some. When Conyers' bill was first introduced in 2003, it had 25 co-sponsors, but that number rose to 88 by the time of its 2009 incarnation. Beautiful in its simplicity, it can be summed up in three words: Medicare for All—just as Mitt Romney believed before he had to satisfy those Tea Party crowds. Sadly, the Conyers bill was too progressive for both Republicans and Democrats. That is one reason why I'm a liberal first, a Democrat second.

Yet another Democratic president, Bill Clinton, worked to provide health care for all Americans and, like his predecessors, was thwarted by lobbying groups and conservative politicians. He was, however, able to get passed the Health Insurance Portability and Accountability Act of 1996. This makes it easier for Americans to keep insurance if they lose their jobs and enables many with preexisting conditions to maintain their insurance policies. Under President Clinton, new protections were put in place for 25 million Americans.

While Bill Clinton's more ambitious plans for medical reform didn't succeed, every American owes him a debt of gratitude for 1993's Family and Medical Leave Act. Were it not for this landmark law, you would stand to lose your job if you or a family member were to get sick. If you've worked in a company with more than 50 e mployees for a year, and you've accrued 1,250 hours of work at your job, you're entitled to take 12 weeks off for illness or to care for a sick family member without being fired or harassed or losing benefits. Until this law was passed, it was up to an employer whether or not to grant time off for medical necessity, and workers could be fired for doing so.

Overlooked in the history of efforts to improve health care is the plan of that great liberal president, Richard Nixon. You might laugh at applying the word *liberal* to the man who famously walked on a beach in a suit and tie, but it was Richard Nixon who introduced the Comprehensive Health Insurance Act that would have required employers to buy health insurance for employees and would have created a Medicaid-type program open to all Americans, who would pay on a sliding scale. Ted Kennedy opposed this measure because it didn't help enough Americans, a stance he later came to regret when he realized it would have been a huge step in the right direction. And, yes, Richard Nixon would be considered a liberal today, as would Ronald Reagan, Gerald Ford, and likely George H. W. Bush. None of them would be welcome at a Tea Party rally, and you have to wonder if they were running today, would they be apologizing for their earlier, liberal positions. Again the name Mitt Romney comes to mind.

Wars of nations are fought to change maps. But wars on poverty are fought to map change. *~Muhammad Ali*

Everyone wishing to be president must either be sympathetic to the poor or at least be able to fake it. Mitt Romney's blow-off, "I'm not concerned about the very poor. We have a safety net there, and if it needs repair I'll fix it," isn't quite up there with Bill Clinton's "I feel your pain." Successful presidents like Bill Clinton do more than feel our pain; they ease it. Sometimes, the pain is so acute that it requires a president to take immediate action. Franklin Roosevelt's New Deal—an astoundingly liberal plan—helped America recover from the Great Depression. This plan focused on what were called the Three R's: Relief, Recovery, and Reform. That meant relief for the poor, recovery from bad economic times, and needed reforms so a similar fate couldn't happen again.

The Civilian Conservation Corps put unemployed, unmarried young men to work in rural areas, with most of their income going to their parents to help their families. Three billion trees were planted to reforest the country, and 800 parks were built, and roads were constructed in rural areas. The Works Progress Administration provided 8 million jobs, putting Americans to work building roads, constructing bridges, and distributing food, clothing, and housing. Almost every community in the United States has a structure built because of the WPA. The Merritt Parkway in Connecticut, the Griffith Observatory in Los Angeles, and the Timberline Lodge on Mt. Hood in Oregon are just a few of them. Many firehouses, libraries, and water mains exist because of this program. Much of the WPA was shut down during World War II by a group called the Conservative Coalition, believing that full employment rendered it no longer necessary. However, many parts of the New Deal live to this day and have helped create a fair and just society.

For example, Roosevelt helped shore up the economy with the Wealth Tax Act, which brought in money from increased inheritance and corporate taxes, a gift tax, and a graduated income tax that made certain the rich paid their fair share. Complain all you want about taxes, but then explain how to pay for the roads, bridges, schools, and the military that conservatives, in particular, love to fund. Tax the rich? It's like what Willie Sutton supposedly said when asked why he robbed banks: "That's where the money is."

The New Deal also brought about the Federal Deposit Insurance Corporation, which makes sure that money you put into a bank account is protected. The Rural Electrification Administration built the electrical infrastructure for rural areas of the United States that big utility companies didn't want to serve. Poor farmers were helped by the Tennessee Valley Authority in obtaining that electricity. The TVA also developed fertilizers and worked to improve crop yields. The Food Stamp Plan, now known as the Supplemental Nutrition Assistance Program (SNAP), created in 1939, then reintroduced in 1961, is still a bone of contention with conservatives and became an issue during the 2012 presidential race. While we're not proud that so many Americans need the food-stamp program, we should be very proud that it exists. At the peak of its four-year initial run between 1939 and 1943 it fed 20 million people. As of 2010, 1 in 7 households—17.2 million homes in the United States— was considered food insecure; thankfully, this government net is there to help these needy families.

Another program that would likely be DOA today but was a key component of FDR's New Deal is Social Security (or Old-Age, Survivors, and Disability Insurance). Like much of the health-care reform that is labeled as a "takeover by the government," this piece of legislation provided care for many people who needed a safety net. Social Security keeps an estimated 40 percent of over-65 Americans above the poverty line. This program helps retirees, those with disabilities, and families who lose a loved one. There were 56 million beneficiaries in 2011. Changes over the years gave more benefits to women, who were not treated as equals in the original plan as they were not as big a part of the workforce, and new categories of workers have become eligible for the program's benefits.

And Roosevelt didn't stop with the New Deal. In order to prevent creating a larger welfare state, he recognized the need to take care of veterans of World War II and signed the G.I. Bill in 1944. Because of this, returning service members were entitled to a high school, vocational school, or college education and a year of unemployment compensation. They were also given the opportunity to get loans to buy homes and get advice about starting businesses. Over the years, various pieces of legislation built upon this manner of taking care of those who serve, as the VA continues to help returning veterans set up businesses, receive job counseling, and purchase group life insurance. And in 2007, Virginia Senator James Webb introduced the Post-9/11 Veterans Educational Assistance Act to give modern-day veterans the same benefits their predecessors had after World War II. Veterans are now eligible for a college education at state schools, including tuition, book money, and a housing allowance.

Another liberal president who helped move our social state forward by responding to the needs of the poor was President Lyndon Johnson, with his plan called the "Great Society." Johnson's War on Poverty, which was part of the Great Society, fundamentally changed the plight of poor Americans and our well-being as a nation. President Johnson appointed Sargent Shriver, who became George McGovern's 1972 running mate, to run the program. The poverty rate dropped from 22.2 percent to 11.1 percent between 1963 and 1973 and has toggled between 11 percent and 15.2 percent since. Among the initiatives of the War on Poverty was VISA, or Volunteers in Service to America, which motivated Americans to get involved in helping address poverty in needy communities, much as the Peace Corps created opportunities to help overseas. While it is much debated how much the government can and should do to help the poor in particular and the economy in general, Lyndon Johnson's Great Society went a long way toward improving the lives of millions of Americans.

The debate about government involvement intensified when the end of the George W. Bush administration brought about the worst economic times since the Great Depression, but there wasn't the will on the part of elected officials of either major political party to do enough quickly enough to rescue the economy. Bush's Troubled Asset Relief Program, or TARP, authorized $700 billion to bail out banks, many of which couldn't have survived without government intervention. Bush was called a bad name for this by his most conservative critics. That name: liberal. President Obama continued to save the economy with the American Recovery and Reinvestment Act, which would have been larger and faster in effect if progressives had had their way. Liberal economist Paul Krugman noted that much of the recovery plan consisted of tax cuts, not the kind of stimulus the government needed to do. "Only about 60 percent of the Obama plan consists of public spending," he explained. "The rest consists of tax cuts—and many economists are skeptical about how much these tax cuts, especially the tax breaks for business, will actually do to boost spending." While the President wanted to do more, the regressives (and I include both Republicans and Democrats in Congress, worried about what they'd tell their constituencies) just wouldn't let him do more. Nevertheless, without both the TARP plan and the Recovery Act, the economy would have plunged even deeper, and American suffering would have been more profound.

What does labor want? . . . We want more schoolhouses and less jails; more books and less arsenals; more learning and less vice; . . . more leisure and less greed; more justice and less revenge . . .
~Samuel Gompers

Here's another way liberals have worked to save America, and this may drive conservatives crazy, but much of what we take for granted today is because of labor unions. Unions are blamed by conservatives for driving up prices, establishing exorbitant pensions, and creating a protected class of lazy workers—plus a host of other ills. But conservatives totally ignore the benefits that they themselves have accrued simply because unions fought for the American worker. I don't think I'm going out on a limb to claim that a large number of American workers are conservative. Yet a powerful upper class and its political allies have worked to reduce union influence, to the point where, according to the Bureau of Labor Statistics, private union membership was just 6.9 percent of the workforce as of 2010, while total membership, public and private, was 11.9 percent and declining. At the height of union popularity in the 1950s, about a third of the workforce belonged to one. By demonizing unions and the workers they represent, and downplaying the real advances that organized labor has made for all Americans, conservatives have been successful in convincing millions of Americans to vote against their own best interests.

Much like the progressives fighting for health care, those at the vanguard of workers' rights were tagged as anti-American. John Kirby of the National Association of Manufacturers said the trade-union movement was "an un-American, illegal, and infamous conspiracy," and there was widespread belief that the American labor movement was attached to the Russian Revolution. Furthermore, our government used its clout to intimidate union leaders. Eugene V. Debs, the first president of the American Railway Union, was put in prison when he organized a strike against the Pullman Palace Car Company, as Attorney General Richard Olney invoked the Sherman Anti-Trust Act. This was the first of Debs's prison sentences. Jailed again in 1918, two years later he conducted his fifth run for president as the Socialist Party candidate from his prison cell.

A cigar maker named Samuel Gompers was another hero of the union movement. He saw that employers were lowering salaries during bad economic times in 1877 and that workers had to organize to claim their rights. Gompers talked about the need for "the elevation of the lowest paid worker to the standard of the highest, and in time we may secure for every person in the trade an existence worthy of human beings." His work with the Cigar Makers Union led to the founding of the American Federation of Labor, which he helmed until his death in 1924. Here are some of the things for which you can thank Mr. Gompers and other early union leaders, such as John L. Lewis, the founder of the Congress of Industrial Organizations:

Weekends. Do you enjoy your weekends? It's nice having a day or two off every week, right? Thank the Amalgamated Clothing Workers of America for fighting, in 1929, for a five-day workweek with Saturdays and Sundays off. Henry Ford had begun shutting his factory down on Saturdays and Sundays in 1926, reasoning it would help worker productivity, and a New England cotton mill made Saturdays a nonworkday to accommodate Jewish workers.

Vacations. How about vacations? Like them? Thank unions, which fought for giving workers paid time off, arguing correctly that it would make them more productive, just as the two-day weekend gave workers time to recharge their engines. Nevertheless, we are still amazingly behind in this area compared to other countries. It was as recent as 2009 that Florida Congressman Alan Grayson introduced the Paid Vacation Act, which would have guaranteed paid time off to American workers, putting them on a par with other industrialized nations. The bill never became law, however, because of objections from conservatives.

Reasonable Hours and Pay. The eight-hour workday is also the result of the labor movement. Labor was in great demand during World War I, and so workers had the clout to make demands. The Adamson Act of 1916 created the eight-hour workday for railroad workers, with overtime pay provided for when they had to put in extra time. You can also thank labor unions for a ceiling on workers' weekly hours and a floor for workers' wages, codified in the Fair Labor Standards Act of 1938. That's when the 40-hour workweek and a minimum wage of 40 cents an hour became law.

The Fair Labor Standards Act also eliminated most child labor. It took another 73 years for someone to object to child labor. During the 2012 presidential race, Fox News analyst Juan Williams questioned Newt Gingrich about his suggestion that African Americans ought to prefer jobs to food stamps and his declaration that we should overturn child labor laws and fire union custodians in schools so we could give jobs to 14-year-olds:

> **Williams:** Speaker Gingrich, you recently said black Americans should demand jobs, not food stamps. You also said poor kids lack a strong work ethic and proposed having them work as janitors in their schools. Can't you see that this is viewed, at a minimum, as insulting to all Americans, but particularly to black Americans?
>
> **Gingrich:** No, I don't see that. (Applause)

I'm guessing that most Americans, members of that debate audience notwithstanding, would rather be productive members of society than recipients of handouts and that most of us like the idea that our children are protected by laws that limit their workplace participation.

Other groups also benefited from the Fair Labor Standards Act, which was amended often, providing more equality as time went on. The 1963 Equal Pay Act banned lower pay based on gender, and the phrase "equal pay for equal work" was born. Farm workers were added to the law in 1966, and age discrimination was outlawed in 1967. A 2007 provision required employers to provide an area in the workplace other than a bathroom where nursing women could breastfeed or express milk.

Key to having achieved these worker gains is the right to collectively bargain, a worker right in existence since the 19th century but recently challenged by Republicans, most notably in Wisconsin. Collective bargaining puts workers on an even playing field with big corporations in the private sector and with powerful government forces in the public sphere. Wages, hours, overtime, safety, and the ability to air grievances have been secured because of this mechanism. The rights of workers to collectively bargain with employers is recognized internationally as a fundamental human right, but when Republican Mitch Daniels became Indiana's governor in 2005, he issued an executive order ending collective bargaining for state employees. When John Kasich became governor of Ohio in 2010, he tried, less successfully, to dismantle collective bargaining. He wanted to take away the right to negotiate on hours, staffing levels, and teacher-student classroom ratios and to forbid public workers from going on strike. Unions were able to garner almost 1.3 million signatures to get a proposal on the 2011 ballot to overturn Kasich's efforts, which had been signed into law with the help of a Republican legislature. What became Issue 2 on the ballot was decided in favor of the unions and against Kasich, leading the governor to wisely proclaim, "It's clear that the people have spoken." Congratulations to the 99 percent.

Wisconsin workers weren't as lucky as those in Ohio. With a Republican governor, Republican House, Republican Senate, and a Republican-dominated Supreme Court, the state took away the right of public unions to negotiate for pay above the rate of inflation and forced them to accept an 8 percent pay cut in pensions, with no right to challenge these changes. Suddenly, after years of fighting for workers' rights, here was one of the biggest assaults on unions in generations. Exempt from these reductions were the police and fire unions, which just so happened to have supported the election bid of Governor Scott Walker. Wisconsin surely had come a long way, in the wrong direction, from the Progressive Era and the governorship of Robert La Follette, who introduced the worker compensation system, which, for the first time, protected workers injured on the job.

We have to remember that Americans have died, not just on the battlefield, but also advocating union efforts that give us the rights we enjoy today. When Chicago's McCormick Reaper Works got wind of a strike in 1886, it locked out all union-card-bearing workers. Police were called when violence erupted, and they opened fire on union workers, killing four of them. At a rally in Haymarket Square to support the workers, a bomb exploded, killing seven officers. Police fired into the crowd, killing even more Americans.

You would think the right to assemble, to speak, and to organize would have been accepted already as key tenets grounded in our Constitution. And yet those introducing new, then-unpopular views sometimes had to pay a fatal price.

After all the battles waged on behalf of the American worker, it's unfortunate that the fight for union representation continues, particularly in those states where progressives are not in power. But let's not forget all the things we enjoy because of what they fought for and continue to fight for.

President Obama once said he wants everybody in America to go to college. What a snob! ~*Rick Santorum*

With a BA from Penn State, an MBA from the University of Pittsburgh, and a JD from Penn State's Dickinson School of Law, Rick Santorum has more degrees than President Obama. But that didn't stop him from trying to impress a conservative audience by suggesting that a Democratic president was an elitist for encouraging Americans to seek education. Mitt Romney also tried to show how elite Obama is by braying that the President had "spent too much time at Harvard." This is remarkable coming from a man who spent more time at Harvard than Obama did: not only does Romney have a law degree and a business degree from Harvard but also he has three sons who went there, and he's donated $50,000 to the university. Romney, a son of privilege, had less of a climb from his roots to the Ivy League than did the son of a Kenyan who didn't grow up in upper-class circumstances.

One thing Santorum's and Romney's remarks did was to reinforce the Right's antipathy for higher education, or at the very least how cynical they can be about it when it serves them politically. By contrast, we can see how much we owe those who've championed education. It's the progressive movement and its leaders in America—people like teacher, education reformer, and New School co-founder John Dewey—who advocated for comprehensive and universal education for our children. Dewey enlightened his era by arguing that education wasn't just about book learning but was a way for children to gain social skills that would serve them in life. Even grander was Dewey's notion that self-fulfillment, as learned in school, would lead to a greater social consciousness and a more democratic way of living. (That's "democratic" with a small "d"; "demo" comes from the Greek *demos*, meaning "people.") Dewey was a modern-day innovator. A citizenry educated through grade 12 is not an old concept. It was only in the 20th century that secondary education became the norm. In 1910, less than 10 percent of teens were in high school, a number that rose to 73 percent by 1940.

Santorum's and Romney's unfortunate comments remind us that seeing higher education as something that should be available to anyone who wants it is also a liberal concept. The United Nations declared in 1966 that "higher education shall be made equally accessible to all, on the basis of capacity, by every appropriate means, and in particular by the progressive introduction of free education." While America has a 99-percent literacy rate above age 15, we rank 10th among industrial countries in the percentage of adults with college degrees. We'd be worse off were it not for the late Rhode

Island Democratic Senator Claiborne Pell, sponsor of the Pell Grant program, which allows financially needy students to go to college. What is little known is that these grants began as help for prisoners, as Pell knew that education while in prison reduced recidivism. "Prisoners' rights" may sound counterintuitive, but a correctional facility can't "correct" without proper education.

In their quest to do away with as much government as they can, conservatives have been pushing to eliminate the Department of Education, seeming not to realize all it does. For one thing, it administers programs that serve low-income students and those with disabilities. It oversees research on our educational system so that we know how well we're doing and can recommend needed reforms. It enforces the law so that there is equal access to education in America for every child, as called for in The Elementary and Secondary Education Act, which was part of Lyndon Johnson's War on Poverty. In this part of the plan, funding was provided so low-income families would have resources equal to those in schools serving wealthier communities. Another part of Johnson's plan included the Jobs Corps, which provided education and vocational training to 16-to-24-year-olds, helping with reading, math, and GED attainment. Today, this program is helping about 60,000 young people. Head Start, one of the most successful and longest-running anti-poverty programs, was a key ingredient in the War on Poverty. Launched in 1964, it initially helped underprivileged preschoolers prepare for kindergarten but was expanded to provide medical, dental, mental health, and nutrition services. The 1964 version of the food-stamp program, which is still in effect, was feeding 46.5 million Americans as of January

2012. The School Breakfast Program, part of the Child Nutrition Act of 1966, has provided more than 100 million children, including 8.1 million children in 2012, hot meals to start their days.

I think the environment should be put in the category of our national security. Defense of our resources is just as important as defense abroad. Otherwise what is there to defend? ~*Robert Redford*

Another target of conservatives is the Environmental Protection Agency, created by the aforementioned liberal, Richard Nixon. I kid, but Nixon would have to be a Democrat today, given his record on a host of issues. You can thank liberals for the EPA's continued existence and its successes. That includes riding hard on air quality, making sure we can breathe easier by cutting down pollution, and making sure that our water is safe to drink. When you open the tap and you don't get sick, thank the EPA. We're protected from radiation caused by nuclear contamination thanks to this agency, which also registers all pesticides sold in the United States.

The EPA also focuses on climate change by promoting energy efficiency and the reduction of greenhouse gasses like carbon dioxide, methane, and nitrous oxide, which, when trapped in the atmosphere, can heat things up. EPA scientists work to keep ecosystems and natural habitats, such as the Great Lakes and Puget Sound, healthy. The agency jumps in when there are natural disasters and emergencies, such as the BP oil spill, where it monitored air, sediment, waste, and dioxin levels. After the 9/11 attacks, the agency, politicized by the Bush administration, was pressured to say that air conditions at

Ground Zero were acceptable, deleting damaging information to make that claim. Had the EPA been allowed to do its job, rescue and cleanup workers would have been able to avoid working in areas that resulted in many of them developing respiratory conditions and contracting cancer, heart disease, and traumatic injuries. As recently as 2011 the New York medical examiner's office added workers exposed to dust at Ground Zero to the death toll.

In giving rights to others which belong to them, we give rights to ourselves and to our country.
~John F. Kennedy

While you're busy thanking liberals (and by now I can feel your gratitude), let's not forget the civil rights movement in America. Civil rights should pertain to any group that is not on an equal playing field in our society. Even though there have been significant victories along the way, the battles for women's rights, rights for African Americans, for Native Americans who were unjustly misplaced, and for gays, continue. Regardless of political affiliation, it's the progressives who have led the way in each case.

The fight for women's rights in America dates back to Elizabeth Cady Stanton, who offered the Declaration of Sentiments and Resolutions at the first women's rights gathering in Seneca Falls, New York, in 1848. Based on the Declaration of Independence, it stated:

> We hold these truths to be self-evident: that all men and women are created equal; that they are endowed by their Creator with certain inalienable rights; that among these are life, liberty, and the pursuit of happiness . . . The history of mankind is a history of

repeated injuries and usurpations on the part of man toward woman, having in direct object the establishment of an absolute tyranny over her. To prove this, let facts be submitted to a candid world.

Listed among the grievances were lack of legislative representation, lack of equality in marital relationships, and lack of property rights. This was the true beginning of the women's suffrage movement, which picked up speed when Stanton and Susan B. Anthony started the National Woman Suffrage Association in 1869. In 1893, Colorado was the first state to adopt an amendment giving women the right to vote, but our Nineteenth Amendment, guaranteeing that right for all women, wasn't ratified until 1920.

Another milestone took place in 1916 when Margaret Sanger, who coined the term *birth control,* opened the first birth-control clinic in Brooklyn, New York, which was shut down ten days later. She was then arrested and convicted for distributing contraceptives but was told she would be granted leniency if she would promise not to break the law again. She refused to make that promise, saying, "I cannot respect the law as it exists today." The trial judge declared that women didn't have "the right to copulate with a feeling of security that there will be no resulting conception." Obviously, the judge was a man.

Interestingly, Sanger's views on race and eugenics were not in line with progressive thought. She believed light-skinned races were superior to those with darker skin (even though she opened a clinic in Harlem to cater to black women) and found common ground with those who believed in stopping the "undeniably feeble-minded" from procreating. These unsavory views are used to argue against her work by those who would like to fully renounce her, but she deserves her due for what she did accomplish for women's rights. Sanger's American Birth Control League eventually became Planned Parenthood, which, to this day, is a target for conservatives because it offers counseling to women on abortion issues. Even though no federal dollars go for this purpose, Planned Parenthood's enemies falsely state otherwise. Lest we think the rights we enjoy today have always been there, it took until 1936 for the government to stop classifying birth control information as obscene, so that information could be sent via federal mail.

President John F. Kennedy appointed Eleanor Roosevelt to head a commission to examine the status of women in 1963, and that contributed to an awareness of discrimination in the workplace because of anti-woman hiring practices, lower pay for women, and the need for maternity leave and affordable day care. This was the beginning of the modern-day women's rights movement, which was further spurred on by Betty Friedan's book *The Feminine Mystique*, wherein she exploded the myth of the happy housewife. This led Friedan to found the National Organization for Women.

When the 1963 Equal Pay Act forced employers to pay equal rates to women for the same work that men did, women made 59 cents on the dollar compared to men. And do you think we've evened the score? Think again. As of 2008, women earn 77 percent of what men do. Libertarians and free-market conservatives believe that it's none of the government's business if an employer wants to pay less to a particular employee and the boss will have to deal with the consequences of his or her own actions. However, this approach doesn't help women, who have historically faced pay discrimination.

It wasn't until 2009 that a little more score-evening took place. Over Republican opposition, President Barack Obama signed the Lilly Ledbetter Fair Pay Act. Lilly Ledbetter, a supervisor at Goodyear Tire and Rubber in Alabama from 1979 to 1998, was paid up to 40 percent less than her male colleagues. Until the passage of this act, you had only 180 days from your *first* discriminatory paycheck to file a complaint. With this new law, victims of pay discrimination can file within 180 days of their *last* paycheck. Republicans, always mindful of protecting big business, were worried that company managers would have to pay the price for discrimination that occurred on the watches of those who no longer worked for a particular firm. Why should they be punished? How about asking why an innocent worker should be punished, which is what Supreme Court Justice Ruth Bader Ginsburg wanted to know. In her dissent in the 2007 case *Ledbetter v. Goodyear Tire & Rubber Co.,* Ginsburg literally invited Congress to correct this injustice, writing, "the Legislature may act to correct this Court's parsimonious reading of Title VII." Here was an example of the court's political divide, with the more liberal justices all agreeing that the court's decision, led by its conservative majority, was a bad one. Luckily, two years later, Congress took Justice Ginsburg's advice and legislated this decision away, giving President Obama the new law to sign. I interviewed Ms. Ledbetter in April 2012 and asked her if she had ever envisioned herself becoming such an iconic figure—one responsible for such an important move forward for women's rights. Her response: "I certainly did not, and I never started out . . .

thinking that someday I would have my name on a case that would make it to the Supreme Court, and especially never a law that would carry my name; and I am so humbled by that recognition alone."

In this country American means white. Everybody else has to hyphenate. ~*Toni Morrison*

Landmark legislation giving equal rights to African Americans was successful because of the work of liberals. Whenever the issue of equal rights comes up, those who oppose evening the score claim that the group seeking parity wants "special rights." Anthony Kennedy addressed this in 1996's *Romer v. Evans,* where the Supreme Court ruled that Colorado couldn't amend its constitution to stop towns and cities from legislating equal rights for gays. Kennedy wrote, "The amendment imposes a special disability upon those persons alone. Homosexuals are forbidden the safeguards that others enjoy or may seek without constraint." In other words, everyone deserves equal protection under the law. It's not "special" to ensure that a particular group has rights equal to what another already has.

Conservatives love to point out that without Republican support, the 1964 Civil Rights Act and the 1965 Voting Rights Act could never have passed and that Southern Democrats opposed these changes. They're right. This is not about political party but rather about progressive thinking, which has historically moved America in the right—er, make that correct—direction. Southern Democrats, known as Dixiecrats, defected from the party in 1948, when Democratic President Harry Truman desegregated the military and Democrats put a civil rights plank in their platform. Thirty-five southern Democrats walked out of that year's convention and formed the States' Rights Democratic Party, with South Carolina Governor—and until then, Democrat—J. Strom Thurmond as its nominee. In fact, a higher percentage of Republicans supported the 1964 Civil Rights Act than did Democrats. But Democrat Thurmond permanently became a Republican when that piece of legislation passed. In that era, it was the North that was progressive, regardless of party, and the South's politicians who were unable to bring themselves to vote for equal rights for blacks.

The Civil Rights Act may have been supported by Republicans, but it had its origins in a June 1963 speech by President John F. Kennedy, who spoke of the need for equality in public accommodations. After Kennedy's assassination, it became a priority of the new Democratic President, Lyndon Johnson, and Kennedy's concept was broadened to include barring unequal application of voter-registration requirements and discrimination based on race, color, religion, or national origin in hotels, restaurants, theaters, and all other places of public accommodation. Access to public government facilities could not be denied, schools were desegregated, a Civil Rights Commission was established, and government agencies that received federal funds could have those monies withheld if they were found to discriminate.

Building upon the Civil Rights Act, the Voting Rights Act of 1965 gave blacks voting equality. Literacy tests and poll taxes, which had been used in Southern states to keep African Americans away from the polls, were outlawed. States with histories of discrimination couldn't make changes to voting laws without clearance from the Department of Justice. In 2006, during a debate on its renewal, some Republicans wanted to eliminate this enforcement provision but, thankfully, were overruled.

One key element of civil rights that is too often overlooked is the Civil Rights Act of 1968. This is also known as the Indian Civil Rights Act, and it made sure that the Bill of Rights was applied within tribes and outlawed discrimination in the sale, renting, and financing of housing. Until this law was enacted, the more than 550 independent Indian nations could be denied jury trials and freedom of the press. Searches and seizures were commonplace in these communities. Finally, Native Americans had legal and constitutional protection.

Another hallmark of the civil rights era had its roots in the Kennedy administration. Equal opportunity for African Americans who had previously been denied it was formally offered via what became known as "affirmative action." The phrase was first mentioned by President Kennedy in 1961, in Executive Order 10925, which created the Committee on Equal Employment Opportunity. Under this order, projects financed with federal dollars had to "take affirmative action" to make sure there was no racial bias in hiring. It was President Johnson who, in September 1965, enforced affirmative action with Executive Order 11216, which required government contractors to "take affirmative action" with regard to minority employees when hiring. Conservatives have historically argued that simply providing equality is enough and we don't have to be proactive by giving what they call "special treatment" to a group once they have equal rights. Lyndon Johnson, speaking at Washington's all-black Howard University in 1965, gave this argument its best rebuttal:

But freedom is not enough. You do not wipe away the scars of centuries by saying: "Now you are free to go where you want, and do as you desire, and choose the leaders you please."

You do not take a person who, for years, has been hobbled by chains and liberate him, bring him up to the starting line of a race and then say, "You are free to compete with all the others," and still justly believe that you have been completely fair. Thus it is not enough just to open the gates of opportunity. All our citizens must have the ability to walk through those gates. This is the next and the more profound stage of the battle for civil rights. We seek not just freedom but opportunity. We seek not just legal equity but human ability, not just equality as a right and a theory but equality as a fact and equality as a result.

Vestiges of racism still exist, even with America's first black president. (A number of callers to my radio show love to remind me that Barack Obama is half white. It's as though they are clinging to a great half-white hope—and to the past.)

Obama built upon the work of his predecessors and enabled further racial parity with the Fair Sentencing Act, which eliminated the mandatory sentence for crack cocaine and eliminated the disparity in sentencing between crimes related to crack cocaine and those involving powder cocaine, as African Americans were often given harsher sentences for the former.

I was raised around heterosexuals, as all heterosexuals are. That's where us gay people come from—you heterosexuals. ~*Ellen DeGeneres*

Calling gay rights a civil rights issue riles some conservatives. They defy comparisons to the struggle for equal rights for African Americans, reasoning that blacks can't change what they are but gays can. I enjoy asking my conservative friends who think this way just when it was that they decided to become heterosexual. Was it a result of peer pressure? Or maybe they saw so much straight television programming that they thought liking the opposite sex was "normal"? Why anyone would "choose" to be gay in an environment where, sadly, it is often still socially unacceptable, is another question they can't answer. Bottom line: it *is* a civil rights issue.

Here are a few more questions: Should a politician or anyone not in a particular relationship decide what a family is? Should "family values" apply only to homes where there is a mother, a father, and 2.57 children? Thankfully, the New York State Supreme Court beat social conservatives to the punch with *Braschi v. Stahl*. Miguel Braschi lived in New York City in a rent-controlled apartment with his partner, Leslie Blanchard. When Blanchard died, the landlord, Stahl and Associates, wanted Braschi evicted because his name wasn't on the lease. In New York, a rent-controlled apartment is even rarer than a parking spot, and when they become vacant a landlord can get market value for a property. A trial court concluded that the relationship between Blanchard and Braschi "fulfills any definitional criteria of the term 'family,'" even though when the rent-control law was written in the 1940s, homosexuality was illegal. An appellate court reversed the trial court, but the state's Supreme Court reversed the appellate court, and family was thus redefined—and for the better.

my job. My question is, under one of your presidencies, do you intend to circumvent the progress that's been made for gay and lesbian soldiers in the military?" Santorum jumped in to say, "Any type of sexual activity has absolutely no place in the military." Oh really? Should we court-martial men and women for holding hands? Again, it's progressives on the right side of history here. Gays can now serve openly in the military, and it's only a matter of time before marriage equality, like equality in the military, will exist nationwide, so that a marriage in Vermont will be recognized in Wyoming. Only then can we truly be the *United* States.

So liberals have been the ones who've fought for the laws that have moved us forward as a nation. But laws can be challenged and changed, as we've seen with the *Lawrence v. Texas* case, the Lilly Ledbetter Act, and the overturning of *Bowers v. Hardwick.* The ability to do this is a good thing because not every law or every court decision is a good one. And no one branch of government should hold sway over the other two. Also, it's important that when a controversial law survives a court challenge, its standing is affirmed and, after a time, becomes an intrinsic part of who we are. Even the regressives who abhor progress eventually arrive at the last stage of grief: acceptance.

A LITTLE HELP TO FIGHT THE RIGHT

Medicaid, Medicare, Social Security, vacations, weekends, a minimum wage, and protected bank deposits barely scratch the surface of reasons to thank a liberal today.

The Affordable Care Act will get rid of coverage denial due to preexisting conditions and lifetime limits on how much coverage you'll have.

Obamacare does not include "death panels," health-care rationing, or coverage for illegal immigrants and abortions, contrary to what you may have heard.

Many of the ideas for health-care reform now opposed by the Right, such as expanded government coverage and mandates, were originally proposed by Republicans.

Raising Americans out of poverty has been a calling card of the Left.

Franklin Roosevelt's New Deal programs like the Civilian Conservation Corps and the Works Progress Administration put Americans back to work after the Great Depression. Almost every community in the United States has structures built because of these programs.

Lyndon Johnson's War on Poverty cut the poverty rate in half. His Jobs Corp provided education and vocational training; Head Start provided medical, dental, mental health, and nutrition services to school children; food stamps have fed tens of millions of hungry Americans.

The Environmental Protection Agency was started by Richard Nixon, whose domestic policies were often liberal. They make sure the air we breathe and the water we drink are healthy. They clean up national disasters such as the BP oil spill and address national tragedies such as 9/11.

Equal pay for women, civil rights for African Americans, and marital rights for gays are hallmarks of the Left. The Lilly Ledbetter Act, the Civil Rights and Voting Rights acts, and the growing number of states permitting marriage equality are thanks to progressives.

Virtually every advancement has occurred because of liberal initiatives and in spite of conservative opposition.

CHAPTER THREE

PROGRESS AFFIRMED!

By now I'm sure you are profusely thanking liberals for consistently being on the right side of history. As in *Lawrence v. Texas*, the rights we take for granted, such as sexual privacy, have often been affirmed by liberal Supreme Court decisions. Our founders must have known what they were doing, as the Constitution has been amended only a handful of times. That is remarkable, considering the changes in technology and lifestyle that have taken place during our almost 300-year history. There have, however, been landmark decisions that have set new precedents or reinterpreted existing law, a necessary flexibility built into our system, given changing times. These decisions most often come from the Supreme Court, although in rare cases a court of appeals may have a ruling in this category when the higher court declines to weigh in on its work.

When a decision comes down that a particular group doesn't like, the jurist is renounced as an "activist judge." But just which judge is an activist depends on which side of an issue you're on. Landmark decisions, the ones that change precedent, are particularly disturbing to the losing side. Conservatives rail against "liberal activist judges" and liberals do the converse when a case doesn't go their way. For example, each side has claimed that decisions about the individual mandate in the Affordable Care Act were made by activist judges. When Judge Henry E. Hudson of U.S. Federal District Court in Richmond called the provision unconstitutional, Bill Scher of the liberal Campaign for America's Future argued that the judge was saying the commerce clause of the Constitution doesn't apply to inactivity—the decision *not* to buy health insurance—thus taking a conservative activist stance. Liberals believe that inactivity in this case *does* affect commerce because of the economic impact caused by those who choose to stay out of a system they will likely eventually enter. The conservative, 5-to-4 decision in *Citizens United v. Federal Election Committee,* the case that defined corporations as people, opened the way for unlimited campaign contributions, a big change from the way things had been. And what was a more activist decision than *Bush v. Gore,* which put a Republican in the White House? But conservatives used to complain that the Earl Warren court was activist, too, given its many progressive decisions. And Warren was a Republican nominated by Republican Dwight Eisenhower.

One of America's earliest landmark decisions was 1803's *Marbury v. Madison,* which gave the Supreme Court the power to strike down laws it considered unconstitutional. But the greatest run of landmark cases came a century and a half later when Earl Warren arrived on the High Court. Warren, a former Governor of California and the 1948 Vice Presidential nominee of the Republican Party (on the ticket with Thomas Dewey), presided over an era of great progress, standing up for the rights of arrested citizens, for keeping government out of our religious lives, and for ending segregation.

Loving v. Virginia, decided in Warren's court, overturned the Racial Integrity Act of 1924, making it legal for people of different races to marry. The case came to the court because in 1958 Mildred Loving, who was black, and Richard Loving, who was white, were arrested for the crime of being married. Under Virginia's Racial Integrity Act, an interracial couple couldn't marry in Virginia or get married legally elsewhere and then come live in that state. The Lovings tied the knot in Washington, D.C., but when they returned to Virginia, police actually raided their home at 2 A.M., hoping to find them having sex so they could arrest them under the state's anti-miscegenation law. The couple was not caught in flagrante delicto, but that didn't stop the authorities from hauling them off to jail. Even being married couldn't save them from arrest.

The Warren court continued to stand up for those who had been denied rights. When an indigent defendant named Clarence Earl Gideon (Do all defendants have three names?) couldn't afford an attorney, he requested one from the court and was denied. After he landed in a Florida state prison on burglary charges, he studied up on the law, found he was right, and wrote a handwritten petition to the Supreme Court to take up his case. It was agreed in 1963's *Gideon v. Wainwright* that even if you couldn't afford it, you had the right to counsel per the Sixth Amendment, which states that "in all criminal prosecutions, the accused shall enjoy the right to . . . have the Assistance of Counsel for his defense." The most vicious, despicable, contemptible felon committing the most heinous act has the right to legal counsel. That is a key ingredient of our judicial system. Until the 1930s, the Supreme Court interpreted this to mean that the government couldn't prevent a defense attorney from participating in a trial. In 1932's *Powell v. Alabama,* it was decided that the state must provide representation in capital trials. Only after the Gideon case was the state required to provide counsel to any defendant accused of a felony who could not afford his own lawyer.

The Supreme Court under Warren also decided that those arrested should have their rights, including the right to an attorney, explained. This is the well-known Miranda warning, decided in 1966 in *Miranda v. Arizona.* After two hours of questioning, Ernesto Miranda signed a confession to a rape and kidnapping. But he was never told he had the right to an attorney or that his statements could be used against him. Lower courts ruled against Miranda, but Chief Justice Warren, writing the opinion of the Court, held that Miranda had been coerced and that his Fifth Amendment right against self-incrimination had been violated. Three justices dissented, arguing that Warren and the court's majority were creating new Constitutional rights that did not previously exist.

This ruling stood as decided until 2010, when a much more conservative court narrowed the decision in *Berghuis v. Thompkins,* stating that now arrestees had to explicitly declare that they wished to remain silent. But it was Warren's view that the Constitution demanded that more be done to protect the accused. In the same spirit, Warren ruled in *Mapp v. Ohio* that prosecutors couldn't use evidence seized in illegal searches. In this case, police believed that a woman named Dollree Mapp and her daughter were harboring a fugitive, and they forced their way into her Ohio home over her protests. When she demanded to see a warrant, they waved a piece of paper at her. Once inside, they cuffed her feet and looked all over the house, but no fugitive was found. However, they arrested Mapp for pornographic material they discovered in her basement. Her bravery led to a decision that state courts, like federal courts, could not use illegally obtained evidence to convict someone. So just in case you ever get arrested and the government tries to frame you, thank liberals that illegally obtained evidence can't be used against you in court.

Our rights to be safe in our homes were further expanded, though not under Justice Warren, in the 2006 case of *Georgia v. Randolph*. It was decided that if the police want to search your home without a warrant, the search can't happen if even one occupant objects.

Warren's best-known decision was one of his earliest ones: *Brown v. Board of Education,* the 1954 case that once and for all affirmed that separate could not be equal, upending what had been the standing rule since *Plessy v. Ferguson* was decided in 1896. In *Brown v. Board of Education,* the Court decided that the Equal Protection Clause of the Fourteenth Amendment meant that separate schools for different races could not coexist. The Warren court continued to make history with cases like *Engel v. Vitale.* Justice Hugo Black wrote the majority opinion that a government-written school prayer violates the Establishment Clause of the

First Amendment. This decision led to others, such as *Wallace v. Jaffree* in 1985, where the Supreme Court said it was unconstitutional for Alabama to set aside a minute for silent prayer or meditation. Religious forces continue to attempt to get their version of God into public schools, but they keep getting shot down by justices who know that this is not in keeping with our government-free religious heritage.

Warren served on the court until 1969, much to the chagrin of conservatives who tried to have him impeached. Yet it is his legacy that gives us so many of the rights we enjoy today. One thing we've learned about Supreme Court appointees is that they don't always reflect the view of the president responsible for putting them there. Two prime examples of this are Justice Sandra Day O'Connor, appointed by Reagan, and John Paul Stevens, a Gerald Ford appointee. In fact, Stevens, until his 2010 retirement, was the most liberal member of the court. He didn't start out that way, however, and throughout his career he considered himself a judicial conservative.

Over time, however, he began to take more liberal positions, and Walter Dellinger, acting Solicitor General in the Clinton administration, referred to him as "the Chief Justice of the Liberal Supreme Court." Once a critic of affirmative action, Stevens voted with the majority to uphold the affirmative action policy at the University of Michigan Law School in *Grutter v. Bolliner,* and O'Connor wrote for the majority that there was a compelling interest in promoting class diversity. O'Connor was another Republican appointee who often voted with the liberal block, one more reminder that her sponsor, Ronald Reagan, was far more liberal than today's Republicans would have you believe.

Stevens also became more opposed to the death penalty as time went on and as new technology such as DNA testing showed how wrong some death sentences were. After he retired, he said the one decision he regretted was 1996's *Gregg v. Georgia,* which reaffirmed the legality of the death penalty. Stevens came to see that putting citizens to death violates the Eighth Amendment's ban on cruel and unusual punishment.

Even when a case is not won by the liberal faction of the Court, I'd like to believe that a strong dissent can have a positive, progressive impact, if only to warn us about going down a dangerous path. Liberal lion John Paul Stevens was known as much for his dissenting opinions as for his concurring ones. Those dissents could be scathing, as when he vigorously opposed the involvement of the U.S. Supreme Court in what should have been a state issue. The case was *Bush v. Gore*, where for the first time ever (and, hopefully, the last), the Supreme Court decided who would be the next president of the United States. Stevens wrote: "One thing, however, is certain. Although we may never know with complete certainty the identity of the winner of this year's presidential election, the identity of the loser is perfectly clear. It is the Nation's confidence in the judge as an impartial guardian of the rule of law." If we're lucky, this warning, courtesy of a dissent, will forever keep the Supreme Court out of deciding elections and prevent the comingling of two branches of government.

Our rights to privacy and other constitutional guarantees must be considered and upheld in light of ever-new technology. This is why the Constitution is less a staid, inflexible document and more a living, breathing one, always intended to be interpreted during changing times. In January 2012, for example, the Supreme Court decided that authorities can't put a GPS device on your car to track your movements without a warrant. Doing so violates the Fourth Amendment prohibition of unreasonable searches and seizures. Of course, who could have foreseen GPS devices in 1776? Here was a case where a conservative Supreme Court did the right thing—really the liberal thing—against the wishes of the usually more progressive Obama administration. The court ruled to uphold the right to privacy, with Justice Samuel Alito acknowledging the factor of technological advancements: "The availability and use of these and other new devices will continue to shape the average person's expectations about the privacy of his or her daily movements."

Other notable cases decided by liberal majorities that have moved this country forward deserve some mention. Your right to privacy—often referred to as "the right to be left alone"—is largely thanks to Estelle Griswold and C. Lee Buxton. Griswold was Executive Director of the Planned Parenthood League of Connecticut, and Dr. Buxton was a physician who taught medicine at Yale. Together, they opened a birth control clinic in New Haven to test a law banning the use of "any drug, medicinal article, or instrument for the purpose of preventing conception." In other words, contraception was illegal. Justices John Marshall Harlan II and Byron White believed that Connecticut's law violated the Fourteenth Amendment's due process clause, and Justice Arthur Goldberg cited the Ninth Amendment, which states that just because a right isn't enumerated in the Constitution, doesn't mean it doesn't exist. The majority opinion by William O. Douglas said that the right to privacy exists in the "penumbras" and "emanations" of the Constitution, meaning it is inherent.

Griswold led to the decision in *Roe v. Wade* that a woman's right to privacy grants her the right to make a decision to have an abortion. Jane Roe, who we now know is Norma McCorvey, was urged by friends to falsely claim she was raped, which would have permitted her to have a legal abortion in Texas. The plan didn't work, and the abortion clinic she was going to visit for an illegal abortion had been closed down. McCorvey won her case, although she later regretted it after anti-abortion activist Flip Benham persuaded her that her previous position was wrong. The legal basis for the *Roe v. Wade* decision has been much-debated, even among those who agree with the result. But it is because of this decision that women aren't sneaking around to unsafe clinics to be manhandled by butchers, and it is because of *Roe v. Wade* that women are no longer self-aborting in ways that cause them to bleed to death.

A few other cases deserve honorable mention, *Schenck v. the United States* for one. Charles Schenck, then secretary of the Socialist Party, distributed leaflets urging people to avoid the draft. The Court decided this violated the Espionage Act of 1917. Expressing the majority opinion that no right is absolute, Justice Oliver Wendell Holmes, Jr., wrote, "The most stringent protection of free speech would not protect a man falsely shouting fire in a theater and causing a panic." Often misquoted, this passage spawned the old canard that no one has the right to shout "Fire!" in a crowded theater. Over the years, the Court eased up on its First Amendment prohibitions, just as the right to bear arms in the Second Amendment went through changes. The Miller decision in 1939 ruled that a sawed-off shotgun did not fall under Second Amendment protection, as it was not something that typically would be used by a "well-regulated Militia." Gun rights have since been expanded, though, as in the 2008 decision in *District of Columbia v. Heller,* which states that the right to a firearm is unrelated to service in a militia.

Larry Flynt is often cited as a First Amendment hero. During a 1976 obscenity trial in Gwinnett County, Georgia, Flynt and his attorney, Gene Reeves, Jr., were shot by a white supremacist who was outraged by a photo of an interracial couple in Flynt's *Hustler* magazine. The shooting left Flynt permanently paralyzed. He was not silenced, however, and in fact became more of a public figure, particularly when he took on Moral Majority founder Jerry Falwell in a 1983 parody. Campari ran a series of ads with famous people talking about their "first time" enjoying the beverage. Flynt portrayed Falwell's first time as involving an incestuous act with his mother in an outhouse while both were "drunk off our God-fearing asses on Campari." Falwell sued, and the Supreme Court heard the case, deciding that no reasonable person could have believed what Flynt wrote was factual. So the Supreme Court agreed that it's okay to have a sense of humor. Flynt's fight to uphold the First Amendment was chronicled in the movie *The People vs. Larry Flynt.*

Larry Flynt is a hero to some, a reprehensible human being to others. But the reason we need a First Amendment is to protect even the most reprehensible speech. That is why First Amendment purists celebrate the 1989 decision in *Texas v. Johnson*. Gregory Lee "Joey" Johnson was a member of a group called the Communist Youth

Brigade who participated in a protest during the 1984 Republican Convention in Dallas. A fellow demonstrator gave Johnson an American flag, which Johnson proceeded to douse with kerosene and burn. Johnson was convicted of desecration of a venerated object, given a year in prison and a $2,000 fine. The Supreme Court had already decided in previous cases that speech is not confined to verbal expression, and in the Johnson case it ruled that the government "may not, however, proscribe particular conduct *because* it has expressive elements." Once again, and thanks to the liberal elements of the Court, reason and freedom prevailed.

A couple of key cases are particularly meaningful against the backdrop of our "War on Terror." In 2006, the Supreme Court ruled in favor of Salim Ahmed Hamdan, a Yemeni citizen who was Osama bin Laden's bodyguard and chauffeur, who believed that the military commission set to try him was illegal. The Supreme Court agreed, determining in *Hamdan v. Rumsfeld* that military commissions set up by the Bush administration violated both the Uniform Code of Military Justice and the Geneva Conventions. Unfortunately, Congress rushed to pass the Military Commissions Act, which forbade using the Geneva Conventions to claim habeas corpus rights.

Liberals won the day again in *Boumediene v. Bush,* which addressed our use of Guantánamo Bay as a holding area for suspected terrorists. The Bush administration reasoned that since Gitmo wasn't on U.S. soil, constitutional protections wouldn't have to be applied to its detainees. Lakhdar Boumediene, a citizen of Bosnia and Herzegovina, challenged this, and the Court decided in his favor by a narrow majority. Anthony Kennedy wrote the majority opinion declaring that habeas corpus applies to persons held at Guantánamo, and that the parts of the Military Commissions Act suspending habeas corpus were unconstitutional.

We who have gone before have performed an honest duty by putting in the power of our successors a state of happiness which no nation ever before had within their choice. If that choice is to throw it away, the dead will have neither the power nor the right to control them. ~*Thomas Jefferson*

Our country was founded by passionate believers in key concepts that continue to be affirmed hundreds of years later by our courts and legislatures. But Thomas Jefferson understood that living majorities must decide for themselves what courses to follow. The particulars may change as they must with shifting circumstances, but the principles stay the same. We are able to apply the thinking of our forefathers to ever-changing times, and that is the beauty of their brilliance. The concepts of habeas corpus, the right to privacy, and equality for all, have played themselves out even as situations our founders could never have anticipated have come to light. Workers' rights, gay marriage, reproductive rights, care for the needy, and all of the advances mentioned in these pages are in keeping with the vision our forebears brought to America.

We battle, we debate, we elect, and move from left to right and then, thankfully, back again. Progressives can't move forward fast enough, and regresssives can't slam on the brakes fast enough. However, progress marches on in spite of those who stand in its way, and because of those who are willing to take chances, sometimes with their lives. We should take comfort, for what we have seen in our short existence as a country is that over time, both legislatively and judicially we come out on the right side of history. Make that the left side of history.

A LITTLE HELP TO FIGHT THE RIGHT

When Congress has been challenged on legislation that's moved the country forward, the courts have mostly upheld these laws. Over time, they've overturned bad laws and reversed bad decisions. *Marbury v. Madison* in 1803 affirmed the court's right to overturn unconstitutional laws.

Lawrence v. Texas overturned *Bowers v. Hardwick* which had made consensual gay sex, even in the privacy of one's own home, illegal. The Lawrence decision paved the way for marriage equality. The Racial Integrity Act of 1924 was overturned by *Loving v. Virginia,* which made it illegal for interracial couples to get married elsewhere and settle in that state.

When Lilly Ledbetter was told by the Supreme Court she couldn't sue for equal pay because the statute of limitations had run out, Congress got to work and gave women more leeway to sue employers who deny them equality.

Other liberal decisions focus on protecting individual rights and include things like an indigent's right to counsel, the right to remain silent when arrested, and the right not to have your home invaded by authorities if anyone in the residence objects. The state can't use illegally obtained evidence against you, and can't put a GPS device on your car to track your movements without a warrant.

The landmark *Brown v. Board of Education* ended school segregation.

Griswold v. Connecticut protects our right to privacy, made birth control legal, and led to legalizing abortion in *Roe v. Wade.*

Larry Flynt's right to mock Jerry Falwell and Joey Johnson's right to burn the flag were upheld, proving the First Amendment is there to protect even the most reprehensible speech.

In *Boumediene v. Bush* it was determined that detainees get constitutional protection, even if they're not on U.S. soil, such as at Guantánamo Bay.

Over time, as Congress legislates progress, the judicial branch tends to affirm it.

CHAPTER FOUR

LIBERAL VALUES ARE AMERICAN VALUES

What's the first thing that comes to mind when you hear the word *liberal?* Uh-oh, something tells me this might not be good. Conservatives say the word as though they've just sucked on a lemon. Even liberals stumble over it, whisper it under their breath, or avoid it entirely in favor of the supposedly less pejorative *progressive.* I'm here to tell you that the word *liberal* has an honorable history, and we should not allow anyone to besmirch it. Righties never seem to be shy about proclaiming that they are conservatives, and liberals have every reason to be equally proud. Women have stood up to "Take Back the Night." Gays have reclaimed a word by calling themselves "Queer Nation." It's about time my side stopped slinking away from the liberal label and all the richness it represents. It's time to claim liberal values as true American values.

As liberals, we must not let conservatives define us. You've heard the myths: Conservatives have family values; liberals don't. Elect Democrats, and they'll reach into women's wombs and kill babies with their bare hands, unless the babies are gay. If the babies are gay, liberals will let them live so they can grow up to become teachers who will turn all their students gay. Add to these misperceptions the canard that liberals want big spending, big taxes, and big government.

Before we get into what liberal values are, let me address what they are not. They are not unpatriotic; they are not immoral; they are not un-American. The knock on liberals that this somehow represents them accounts for one of the reasons some people shy away from the word in the first place.

America is much more than a geographical fact. It is a political and moral fact—the first community in which men set out in principle to institutionalize freedom, responsible government, and human equality. *~Adlai Stevenson*

"American values" is a fungible concept. Conservatives like to define it in terms of freedom and patriotism. Because of this, these words—and many others—have taken on different meanings, depending upon who is using them.

One of the principles that liberals are most often accused of lacking is family values. This phrase has become code for right-wing policies that dictate that marriage is between only a man and a woman, and only

a household consisting of these two figures should be allowed to raise children—no gay households need apply.
However, liberals would argue that *family values* has a
very different meaning. For one thing, people should be
allowed to decide for themselves just what a family con-
sists of. Not every American has the luxury of a mother
and a father. Not every child is wanted. Who should
tell anyone else who it's appropriate to love? (Of course,
we're talking about adults here.) Liberal values concur
with the belief that the validity of a family shouldn't be
based on the number of members, how they love each
other, or the gender of its personnel.

Besides, you'd think that if marriage were so important, its value would hold true for any two consenting
adults. Gay marriage is right in line with values conservatives hold dear. Marriage promotes stability and mo-
nogamy, they say. Well, that applies regardless of which
gender gets to participate in the nuptials. Equally consistent with these values is the right of same-sex couples
to adopt. With tens of thousands of children in America
waiting to be taken in by loving families, it is the opposite of family values not to give them every opportunity to find homes. When confronted by someone who
is against gays adopting, I like to ask them: If there were
a choice between keeping a child in foster care, often
being shunted from home to home, or having her raised
by a gay couple in a stable, loving environment, which
would you prefer?

Freedom is another word that has taken on a conservative tone, but if we look more closely at it, we can
see that freedom also means different things to different people. To a libertarian, it means almost no government and leaving those who can't make it on their

own to suffer whatever fate has in store. During a September 2011 presidential debate, moderator Wolf Blitzer asked candidate Ron Paul about a hypothetical healthy 30-year-old who doesn't have health insurance, suddenly gets sick and falls into a coma.

"Who pays?" Blitzer wanted to know.

"That's what freedom is all about," said Paul, "taking your own risks. This idea that you have to take care of everybody . . . "

Blitzer: "But, congressman, are you saying that society should just let him die?"

At this point the crowd's libertarian strain was obvious as they cheered, with a number of them letting out a "Yeah!"

Paul, a physician by trade, replied, "No. I practiced medicine before we had Medicaid. . . . We never turned anybody away from the hospitals. We've given up on this whole concept that we might take care of ourselves and assume responsibility for ourselves. Our neighbors, our church would do it."

To conservatives, freedom might mean promoting their ideas of what a family should be, who your lover should be, when a life begins, and having the most prolific military known to man. It likely means that children should all have mommies and daddies, gays should keep us free from having to deal with their lifestyle, and the rights of a pregnant mother are superseded by the rights of the fetus, which can't defend itself. And freedom must be maintained, they will argue, by putting as much money as we can into the military and weapons systems to scare off would-be attackers.

To a liberal, freedom is attained when the most needy and least empowered among us are protected from those who could do them harm. That generally pertains to already-born humans. We believe that freedom is a woman's right to choose what happens to her body when she becomes pregnant. It means that she can safely visit a doctor or clinic if, for any reason of her choosing, she doesn't wish to bring the fetus to term. Freedom is allowing a doctor and a family, not a politician, to make a decision about the life of a pregnant woman if she is in physical danger. It's making sure that gays who love each other have the same legal rights as straights do if they wish to involve the government in their union. It's allowing gays to adopt children waiting in shelters for loving families. And freedom is having a military scaled to what is necessary, so that money is available for a variety of other, non-military purposes.

The stark difference between conservative and liberal views of freedom was never more evident than in the debate on whether to retain the Affordable Care Act. During the court proceedings, conservatives argued that freedoms were being taken away from Americans by forcing them to buy health insurance they may not want. Liberals turned that argument around to show that by getting all Americans into the game, you lower the incidence of "free riders"—those whose health care is paid for by the rest of us—thus reducing our premiums. That provides more freedom for the taxpayers, who no longer have to support the uninsured. In closing arguments, Solicitor General Donald Verrilli used this argument to try to convince the Supreme Court of the law's validity, reasoning, "There is an important connection, a profound connection, between that problem and liberty, and I do think it's important that we not lose sight of that."

Right up there with freedom as a commonly stated American value is patriotism. To a conservative, this might mean waving the American flag. To a liberal or possibly a libertarian, it's the right to wave it but also to burn it, something the Supreme Court has averred. It was almost comical after 9/11 to see television personalities suddenly show up wearing flag pins, as though putting a flag on a suit shows how much you love America. I was one of them. One day it occurred to me that I didn't need a pin on my lapel to show how American I am. I received some hate e-mail suggesting that not only did I lack patriotism but better Americans wore bigger pins than mine. It was a revelation to learn that when it comes to patriotism, size counts.

President Obama similarly stopped wearing a flag pin the year before he was elected president. An ABC reporter asked him about it, and he replied, "The truth is that right after 9/11, I had a pin. Shortly after 9/11, . . . that became a substitute for, I think, true patriotism, which is speaking out on issues that are of importance to our national security." He was in the important campaign state of Iowa at the time and added, "I decided I won't wear that pin on my chest. Instead I'm going to try to tell the American people what I believe will make this country great, and hopefully that will be a testimony to my patriotism." Obama immediately received withering criticism about his patriotism and then expanded upon his thinking the next day: "After a while, you start noticing people wearing a lapel pin but not acting very patriotic. Not voting to provide veterans with resources that they need. Not voting to make sure that disability payments were coming out on time. My attitude is that I'm less concerned about what you're wearing on your lapel than what's in your heart." One snarky right-wing website wrote, "Maybe at Harvard Law School they don't teach the difference between patriotism and treason." Really? A lapel lacking a pin is treasonous? Get that blogger a thesaurus, quick.

One way some knuckleheads think you can show love for our country is to yell its name at other people. When two men started kissing at a Rick Santorum rally in March 2012, the crowd began chanting, "USA! USA!" They seemingly thought they could overcome gayness with patriotism. Two men kissing? Yell out the name of our country; that'll straighten them out! A couple of weeks earlier, when Alamo Heights, a mostly white Texas high school basketball team beat the mostly minority students from San Antonio Edison, the predominantly white crowd burst into the same "USA! USA!"chant. This time, a loud exhaling of our name was intended to combat those who "looked" foreign.

Even the word *American* has a conservative feel to it. Mark Steyn, no liberal he, pointed out this absurdity in the *National Review,* mocking Mitt Romney by satirically suggesting what the presidential candidate might say in a stump speech: "I believe in an America where millions of Americans believe in an America that's the America millions of Americans believe in. That's the America I love." I don't think Amerigo Vespucci, from whom our country got its name, ever used his own monicker as often in such a short time frame.

During the 2008 presidential campaign, Sarah Palin told a cheering crowd how much she loved being in the "pro-America areas" of America, declaring,

> We believe that the best of America is not all in Washington, D.C. We believe—we believe that the best of

America is in these small towns that we get to visit and in these wonderful little pockets of what I call the real America, being here with all of you hardworking, very patriotic, um, very, um, pro-America areas of this great nation. This is where we find the kindness and the goodness and the courage of everyday Americans. Those who are running our factories and teaching our kids and growing our food and are fighting our wars for us. Those who are protecting us in uniform. Those who are protecting the virtues of freedom.

If there were a language police, Palin's rhetoric would get one arrested for word abuse. Let's make a salad of words that sound important. We'll use *America, American, goodness,* and *kindness.* We'll toss in *uniform, virtue,* and *courage.* Oh, and let's add a pinch of *fighting our wars* and *protecting.* And please don't forget the main ingredient: *freedom!* Better not use any French or Russian dressing on that salad.

Go tell the mom raising her kids in the nation's capital that she's not the good part of America. Tell the dad who lost his son in Iraq or Afghanistan that it doesn't count as much because he's not from a small town. Explain to the Good Samaritan New York cabbie that the billfold he returned to a customer isn't as good an act of kindness as a similar deed performed by an Iowa farmer.

This separation of real-versus-fake Americans is a theme Republicans began using in 1984, when former U.N. Ambassador Jeanne Kirkpatrick blamed "San Francisco Democrats" for a "blame America first" mentality at the Republican National Convention. If you're blaming an entire major American city for some perceived monolithic belief, aren't *you* a member of the "blame America first" crowd? In 1996, Congressman Frank

Riggs of California's 1st District accused his Democratic opponent, Michela Alioto, of having "San Francisco values." No wonder Riggs's later attempt to run for the U.S. Senate fizzled. How can you claim to represent a state when you've insulted so much of it? When Nancy Pelosi became the Speaker of the House, the term *San Francisco values* came back into vogue with those who considered themselves better Americans than San Franciscans. Pelosi, no fan of predecessor Newt Gingrich, said "there's something I know" in reference to the former Speaker, implying some secret would ruin his presidential aspirations. Pelosi later clarified her remarks, stating that what she knew was that Newt Gingrich would not become president of the United States. Gingrich responded to Pelosi's initial statement on the *Today* show, saying she "lives in a San Francisco environment of very strange fantasies and very strange understandings of reality." Listening to these GOPers you'd think that, in the words of *SFist* editor Brock Keeling, San Francisco is "Baghdad by the Bay."

Can one of these anti–San Francisco Americans explain to the family of Lieutenant Vincent Perez that he represents a part of America that isn't as valid as the small towns Sarah Palin extols? Perez, a former Marine and Alameda County sheriff's deputy, served for 21 years in the San Francisco Fire Department before losing his life in June 2011, trying to save a family's home in Diamond Heights. Isn't it amazing that the good work of Lieutenant Perez was achievable in "a San Francisco environment"?

And this non-American criticism has moved beyond just regions of the country. One of the memes running through President Obama's election, presidency, and reelection campaign has been the allegation that he is not one of us; instead, he's foreign, and either a Muslim or the wrong kind of Christian. In a September 2010 *Forbes* article, Dinesh D'Souza accomplished the most vicious takedown of Obama in recent memory, opining: "Incredibly, the U.S. is being ruled according to the dreams of a Luo tribesman of the 1950s. This philandering, inebriated African socialist, who raged against the world for denying him the realization of his anticolonial ambitions, is now setting the nation's agenda through the reincarnation of his dreams in his son." Forget how racist and insulting this is; it's incomprehensible. Yet Newt Gingrich told the *National Review* this was "stunning insight" and "the most profound insight I have read in the last six years about Barack Obama."

Gingrich also said Obama has "a European radical attitude toward class warfare." With that careful wording you can link the president to another culture and country without actually saying he's from there. These opinions are a more intellectualized version of the birthers, who will never agree that Obama is American unless they can time-travel backward and appear in his hospital delivery room.

True American values aren't about pins and flags or whether you have a rural, urban, or suburban zip code. Our founders created this country based on ideas and principles, not on the details surrounding all our actions. I can't recall one mention in the Constitution of men not being able to marry other men or of women not having abortions. I think that both the Left and the Right believe our founders started America as an upright, ethical nation—that is, one with good values. So can we agree that liberals and conservatives both love

America, and that America includes a variety of cities, towns, and hamlets, urban, suburban, and rural? Can we accept that even though my values may be different from yours, this doesn't necessarily make them un-American?

So just what are liberal values that could just as well be called American values?

Whenever the government provides opportunities and privileges for white people and rich people they call it "subsidies." When they do it for Negro and poor people they call it "welfare." ~*Martin Luther King, Jr.*

The great divide between left and right that informs how we think about so many issues is what role government should play in our lives. Liberals tend to have a more positive view of what government can accomplish, while the Right loves to denounce anything that reeks of "Big Brother." Funny how the anti-government sentiment by conservatives never seems to apply to that big government bureaucracy called the Pentagon or to government intrusion into a woman's womb.

For years, conservatives have promoted the old wives' tale that government is the enemy and that liberals are so in love with bureaucracy that they want to control everyone's life. But it's not that liberals want bureaucracy; it's that we believe in providing a fair playing ground for all citizens. We don't look at government as an ogre, here to take away our freedoms; we see it as a salve to protect these freedoms. Regulations aren't land mines to squelch entrepreneurship; they're guidelines to enable us to play by the rules, a concept conservatives view as very much in line with their values.

Conservatives might have you believe they're the only thing that stands between a tidal wave of government and freedom. But if you look at history, this story just doesn't hold water. Both sides—Republican and Democratic—have had presidents with records of raising taxes and increasing the size of government and, certainly, government payrolls. Both sides have also had presidents who have controlled budgets and shown fiscal responsibility. Liberals aren't the pushers of big government they get accused of being, and conservatives aren't always conservative when it comes to government and spending.

Ronald Reagan increased the government payroll by 60,000 jobs by creating the Department of Veterans Affairs. And after he cut taxes, he then had to raise them—11 times, according to former Republican Senator Alan Simpson, co-chair of President Obama's deficit commission. These increases were necessary to make up for money that was no longer coming into the U.S. Treasury. Reagan spent $100 billion a year on defense, an unheard of amount at that time, a number that helped take our deficit in the Reagan years from $700 billion to almost $3 trillion. Conversely, President Clinton left office with a huge government surplus. And President Obama offered Republicans $2 trillion in spending cuts if they would agree to $400 billion in taxes on the wealthy. That's an 83 to 17 ratio, which the Republicans rejected. They rejected it for one major reason: the person offering it was Barack Obama.

And if bigger government isn't giving bigger eyes to Big Brother, I don't know what is. Witness the Uniting and Strengthening America by Providing Appropriate Tools Required to Intercept and Obstruct Terrorism Act of 2001. You probably know it as the USA PATRIOT Act (and so did I before doing the research for this book). I wonder whose job it was to come up with words that would properly match the initials. Some schnook, likely a legislative aide, had to sit in an office with a thesaurus. Not only does the Patriot Act pack the halls of government but it also moves us away from the ideals of freedom touted by conservatives. It allows "sneak-and-peak" warrants, where authorities can enter private property without permission and tell you after the fact. Also allowed are roving wiretaps, controversial because they don't apply to a particular phone line or e-mail account but can apply to any such platform used by a particular suspect. And the library provision, the infamous Section 215, allows the government to look at "tangible things," notably "books, records, papers, documents, and other items."

Actions of liberals surrounding this very unpatriotic act really exemplify our view of what the government should do. U.S. District Court Judge Ann Aiken declared "sneak-and-peak" unconstitutional in 2007, but unfortunately, her decision was overturned by the Ninth Circuit in 2009. Aiken was attempting to change the government from being what conservatives say they fear—Big Brother—back into the mechanism that protects the freedoms of all Americans. Contrary to its advance advertising, the Patriot Act hasn't been used just to go after terrorists. In 2003, for example, the government used Section 215 to look at the records of a strip-club owner in Las Vegas and politicians he allegedly paid off. Somehow, I doubt topless dancers offer the same threat as terrorists steering planes into tall buildings.

Ronald Reagan joked that one of the great American lies is, "I'm from the government, and I'm here to help you." And this is truly what liberals believe—that the government is here to help all of us, not just minorities, the poor, gays, immigrants, and those accused (sometimes falsely) of crime. Of course we know that the Right believes these groups are, in aggregate, the Democratic base. Martin Luther King, Jr., was correct that government's role is regarded very differently when it's the wealthy who are the beneficiaries. It's a reminder that we have to hand it to the right wing in their ability to frame arguments.

Let's not forget that government favoritism extends to right-leaning groups as well. Tax breaks for oil companies and loopholes that allow offshore storing of assets are just a couple of ways government works for the wealthy. But the poor need more from the government than the rich do. Good for Mitt Romney that he is permitted to store millions in assets in Cayman Island tax havens, but he'd do just fine without that bit of government largess. Government isn't the enemy; its employees aren't automatically incompetent (another broad generalization that has played itself out with the attack on public unions); and when the government steps in to regulate something, it isn't fascism. Our heroic first responders are government workers. Our police, fire, and military workers keep us safe and protected. Government regulations make sure that when you bite into a potato chip you don't die of arsenic poisoning and that when you get into your car the engine doesn't explode. I could go on and on, but you get the idea—and this is why liberals believe that government isn't the boogeyman conservatives make it out to be.

When we apologize, we end our struggle with history.
~John Kador

Aside from the role of government, liberals espouse a number of values that often get them called weak and wishy-washy. Values like recognizing and acknowledging—even apologizing for—past mistakes. Values like changing a stance based on new information. Values like forgiveness and humility. I'm not saying conservatives don't also share some of these values, but let's just say that liberals are more often tagged with them—and sometimes mocked for them—especially when they're displayed on a national stage. But rather than invite ridicule, I would argue that they should inspire respect and admiration.

One of the bedrock tenets of liberalism is the ability to change your thinking. You may believe the earth is flat on Monday, but if new evidence comes to light on Tuesday, you change your views. The great orator Daniel Webster said in a speech in 1846, "Inconsistencies of opinion, arising from changes in circumstances, are often justifiable." His contemporary, the orator and abolitionist Wendell Phillips, agreed, stating, "I will utter what I believe today, [even] if it should contradict all I said yesterday." As the British philosopher Bertrand Russell said, "The essence of the Liberal outlook lies not in *what* opinions are held, but in *how* they are held: instead of being held dogmatically, they are held tentatively, and with a consciousness that new evidence may at any moment lead to their abandonment." Having this view of the world does not make us flip-floppers. It merely speaks to our ability to change with the times and live within the constraints of reality. Yes, we liberals proudly admit we are full-fledged members of the "reality-based community," even as that term was used to mock journalist Ron Suskind by a George W. Bush advisor. We don't dig in intransigently without altering a position when new information is available. Opinions can and should change, and not just when it's political season. When a former governor of Massachusetts suddenly offers a new opinion because his new constituency is made up of far-right primary voters and no longer citizens of a blue state, a changing opinion is suspect.

This ability to change opinions brings with it an awareness that not everything we have done as a country is worthy of pride. Conservatives claim that recognizing and acknowledging this makes us look weak. And apologizing? That makes us look even more pathetic—and un-American.

President Obama has been accused of being ashamed of his country, charged with going around the world apologizing for America and appeasing our enemies. Early in the Obama presidency, Former George W. Bush advisor Karl Rove called one such incident "The President's Apology Tour" in *The Wall Street Journal*. Key to his argument was that Obama worked to distance himself from his predecessor, whose arrogance toward other countries he found distasteful. Rove wrote:

> Mr. Obama told the French (the French!) that America "has shown arrogance and been dismissive, even derisive" toward Europe. In Prague, he said America has "a moral responsibility to act" on arms control because only the U.S. had "used a nuclear weapon." In London, he said that decisions about the world financial system were no longer made by "just Roosevelt and Churchill sitting in a room with a brandy"—as if that were a bad thing. And in Latin America, he said

the U.S. had not "pursued and sustained engagement with our neighbors" because we "failed to see that our own progress is tied directly to progress throughout the Americas."

Obama told the French we were arrogant. The French, mind you! Oh, you mean that country that objected to the United States invading Iraq? Yes, that country, the one that turned out to be correct about Iraq. France was so reviled by conservatives when we invaded Iraq in 2003 that Republican congressman Bob Ney of Ohio, in his capacity as Chairman of the House Administration Committee, ordered that all mentions of French fries and French toast in House cafeterias and snack bars be changed to "freedom fries" and "freedom toast." Here we were in a so-called war on terror, and these guys were concerned about what we call potatoes and bread. Given that Ney's political career ended when he pleaded guilty to charges of conspiracy to defraud the United States by taking bribes to help clients of lobbyist Jack Abramoff, he would have been better off spending less time obsessing about how to name food. Yes, the President told the French we were arrogant. But left out of Rove's attack, and omitted by those who've repeated it, is the next line of Obama's speech when he told the French they were, too:

> But in Europe, there is an anti-Americanism that is at once casual but can also be insidious. Instead of recognizing the good that America so often does in the world, there have been times where Europeans choose to blame America for much of what's bad.

It took strength, not weakness, to stand up in front of the world, make the charge of anti-Americanism, and say we could have done things better as well. The traits that enable us to have better interpersonal relationships are the very same values we can use in international relationships to give us a better standing in the world and give the world a better understanding of us.

I also take issue with the notion that "apology" means "weakness." Aren't we taught by our parents to fess up when we've done something wrong? "Stand up and admit it like a man," I was told. Thus, to me, this signifies strength, the very opposite of how it is often portrayed. When we have shown this kind of strength as a nation, it's made us better for it. It has helped us heal and brought us together.

We have recently begun to recognize the horror we visited upon the original occupants of our land. The revolutionaries who founded our country believed they were fighting for freedom, but the Native Americans didn't see it that way. As British author Gerald Seymour wrote, "One man's terrorist is another man's freedom fighter."

We regard our founders as great freedom fighters and the purest Americans who ever existed. But try telling that to a Native American whose land was taken or whose family was murdered at Wounded Knee or Sand Creek. In those tragedies, the U.S. military massacred Native Americans. It wasn't until September 2000, when Kevin Gover, speaking for the Department of Indian Affairs, acknowledged our treatment of those whose land we took:

> This agency forbade the speaking of Indian languages, prohibited the conduct of traditional religious activities, outlawed traditional government, and made Indian people ashamed of who they were . . .

And so today I stand before you as the leader of an institution that in the past has committed acts so terrible that they infect, diminish, and destroy the lives of Indian people decades later, generations later. These things occurred despite the efforts of many good people with good hearts who sought to prevent them. These wrongs must be acknowledged if the healing is to begin.

Gover took responsibility by recognizing an ugly part of our country's past and apologizing for it. And this isn't the only recent incidence of America developing an awareness of despicable past behavior and doing something about it.

In May 1997, President Clinton did something remarkable. He stood up in the East Room of the White House and said the words, "The United States Government did something that was wrong, deeply, profoundly, morally wrong. It was an outrage to our commitment to integrity and equality for all our citizens. We can end the silence. We can stop turning our heads away. We can look at you in the eye and finally say on behalf of the American people what the United States Government did was shameful, and I am sorry." What he was talking about was our government's Tuskegee study, where hundreds of African-American men were lied to about getting free medical care for syphilis when they were actually going untreated to see how the disease would progress. This began in 1932 but wasn't made public until 1972, when Peter Buxtom, a former Health Service worker, leaked the story to the Associated Press. In the interim, 28 men died of syphilis, 100 more died of related complications, at least 40 wives were infected, and 19 children were born with the disease. In 1974 the victims won a $10 million out-of-court settlement, and the court ordered the government to give them free lifetime health care. But it took another 13 years to formally admit this horrific chapter in our nation's history.

In another reprehensible part of our past, the U.S. sterilized women against their will as a result of eugenics laws that were on the books well into the 1970s. The victims were mostly poor, black, uneducated, and incarcerated women, who were deemed "unfit to breed." Also targeted were juvenile delinquents, epilepsy sufferers, the mentally ill, and gay men. Supreme Court Justice Oliver Wendell Holmes, Jr., to his everlasting shame, wrote the majority decision in *Buck v. Bell* in 1927 that enabled this practice. He wrote that the state had a greater interest in creating a pure gene pool than in guaranteeing citizens control of their own bodies.

> We have seen more than once that the public welfare may call upon the best citizens for their lives. It would be strange if it could not call upon those who already sap the strength of the State for these lesser sacrifices, often not felt to be such by those concerned, in order to prevent our being swamped with incompetence. It is better for all the world if, instead of waiting to execute degenerate offspring for crime or to let them starve for their imbecility, society can prevent those who are manifestly unfit from continuing their kind. The principle that sustains compulsory vaccination is broad enough to cover cutting the Fallopian tubes . . . Three generations of imbeciles are enough.

As a result, more than 60,000 Americans were denied their right to reproduce, often without even knowing this was being done to them. North Carolina was one of the biggest offenders among the 32 states who perpetrated this crime against humanity, which ceased in 1979. But it took until 2011 for North Carolina to consider compensating the victims of the heinous practice, and the state began looking for the 2,900 victims believed to still be alive. Under consideration was a $50,000 payout to each victim, as if that weren't a further insult. How do you even put a price on what a government should pay after forcefully and sneakily preventing a human being from being able to reproduce? In 2002, then-Governor Mike Easley apologized, saying, "On behalf of the state, I deeply apologize to the victims and their families for this past injustice and for the pain and suffering they had to endure over the years. This is a sad and regrettable chapter in the state's history, and it must be one that is never repeated again." But in 2011, Governor Bev Perdue went a step further, saying an apology wasn't enough and amends had to be made before those victimized by this policy were no longer around to benefit from it. She urged, "I want this solved on my watch. I want there to be completion. I want the whole discussion to end and there to be action for these folks. There is nobody in North Carolina who is waiting for anybody to die."

This recognition of past mistakes isn't necessarily confined to Democrats. President George H. W. Bush apologized in 1992 to Japanese Americans for the U.S. detaining them in internment camps during World War II. Approximately 110,000 Japanese and Japanese Americans were rounded up and put in "War Relocation Camps" based on an executive order signed by President Franklin Roosevelt. Here you had a Republican President apologizing for something a liberal Democratic president did. In fact, the first acknowledgment of this atrocious episode came from the Republican Gerald Ford, who proclaimed it a "national mistake." Years later, Ronald Reagan signed the Civil Liberties Act of 1988, which provided $20,000 to each surviving detainee. One of the bill's sponsors was Norman Minetta, a California congressman who went on to become Bill Clinton's Secretary of Commerce and George W. Bush's Secretary of Transportation. One can never make right such an egregious wrong, but Gerald Ford, Ronald Reagan, and George H. W. Bush did just what liberals are criticized for by candidly addressing parts of our shameful past.

We can't go back in history and right the wrongs of our past, but having true liberal values means we acknowledge them and do as much as we can to take care of those who suffered.

I am (a Hindu). I am also a Christian, a Muslim, a Buddhist, and a Jew. ~*Gandhi*

In my previous book, *Red, White & Liberal* (available at online bookstores everywhere, and a number of remainder bins), I titled a chapter "Jesus Was a Liberal," much to the consternation of a few anti-liberal malcontents. Truth is, not only was Jesus a liberal—a sandal-wearing, long-haired, love-preaching hippie—but so were most major historical spiritual figures and the religions they represented.

Conventional wisdom is that values and religion are closely aligned. You don't necessarily need religion to have values, and being a religious practitioner certainly doesn't guarantee that you have good values. But if you study the world's great religions, you will notice two main things: first, that they each deliver similar messages and, second, that their teachings are very much in line with liberal thinking. Whether or not you believe Jesus was God, or even whether he existed, is immaterial. The legend of Jesus is that of the ideal human who shows love for all, including his enemies. And while not enough liberals—or anyone else—live up to Jesus's words, I contend that progressive policies are more in line with his teachings than many conservative ones.

Much of the criticism of liberal values comes in the form of claims that we don't live by Christian values. This is demonstrably untrue. You know that Christian phrase "Love thy neighbor as thyself?" This is a phrase liberal policies truly take into account. That means if a neighbor needs a helping hand, some of us who can afford to pay more taxes should help. This means letting our neighbors know when we make a mistake. It means accepting people of all stripes—bi-, gay, straight, black, white, or polka-dotted. They are each, after all, our neighbors. Liberals even believe in loving thy enemies. President Obama was heavily criticized during his first presidential campaign when he said he'd talk to Iran. Candidate Ron Paul echoed this sentiment and was similarly mocked. Bold efforts for direct talks with any of our opponents, no matter how evil they are or were, might have prevented unnecessary wars and saved hundreds of thousands of lives.

And how about one of the most beautiful of Jesus's teachings: forgiveness? As it says in Luke 23:34, "Father, forgive them, for they know not what they do." I know many conservatives who have such contempt for liberals that when they say the L word, it's as though they've just put something in their mouths that they recently stepped in and have to spit it out as quickly as possible.

So if you think my political brethren and I are a bunch of left-wing loons, don't get mad at us. Don't even try to get even. Just have the attitude that we should be forgiven, for we know not what we do.

These Jesus-taught concepts are true liberal ideals for which we all strive. Can you imagine how the world would be if we exhibited these qualities when making policy, when dealing with our enemies, and when dealing with each other? If we were truly the Christian nation the Right believes we are, we'd be following the tenets Jesus preached and we'd truly be the beacon of liberty and morality we purport to be. We'd recognize that loving God and honoring Him would mean being more like Him. As it says in Isaiah, "they will hammer their swords into plowshares and their spears into pruning hooks. Nation will not lift up sword against nation, and never again will they learn war."

These are not Pollyannaish ideas. What Jesus preached is simple but not easy. Doing the right thing too often loses ground to temptation. We seek revenge more often than we seek justice. It feels satisfying to fry criminals who have committed heinous acts because we hunger for revenge. While the search for justice doesn't feel as good in the short run, it's the Christian (and liberal) thing to do. The Catholic Church realizes this, which is why it stands against the death penalty. Shouldn't it be up to God, not politicians, who lives and who dies? But let's move beyond Christianity—just in case you're not won over by Jesus.

Judaism and Islam, Christianity's Abrahamic brothers, both teach that humans are born pure and that all that God created should be treated with equality and compassion. They put forth that we are naturally inclined to do good, even though we also have a tendency to do evil, but there is free will to choose. Thankfully, one can always atone through prayer and repentance and gain forgiveness—true believers in either of these faiths would never support policies such as the death penalty.

One concept central to Judaism—and liberalism—is *Tikkun Olam*, which literally means "world repair." It commands Jews to work toward a model society and improve the world at large by promoting social justice. And Judaism teaches that you need not be a Jew to be righteous; acceptance of others and their own paths is key to the faith. While we're at it, let me straighten this whole thing out about being the chosen people. This is often misinterpreted as meaning that Jews are the fair-haired (okay, curly-haired) pets of God. It actually has more to do with Jews being chosen by God to have to uphold certain morals and responsibilities as an example to the rest of mankind. Hence, the Yiddish playwright Sholem Aleichem's reportedly famous saying, "God, I know we are your chosen people, but couldn't you choose somebody else for a change?"

Islam gets a bad rap in the West, but the truth is, this faith shares the same Judeo-Christian values mentioned here. It is open to all people regardless of background or upbringing. It's one of the world's fastest-growing religions, largely because it is so welcoming. Charitable loving-kindness, concern, and giving to the needy encompass one of the five pillars of Islam. That many Islamic countries are not exactly bastions of liberalism is a political calculus, reflecting social, political, and economic systems more than religious ones. But theologically, Islam offers many teachings that are much in keeping with the values found in most other major religions.

Buddhism, one of the world's largest religions—and another example of liberal values—follows the teaching of Siddhartha, the man who eventually become known as the Buddha. He devoted his life to finding and teaching happiness, and he inspired his followers to reach out with great compassion to all who needed help. The Buddha spoke only kindly to people, never losing his temper or becoming impatient. We could all learn from him, especially those of us who work in talk radio and cable news. Among his tenets is "Whoever serves the sick and suffering serves me." He preached that we are all one, that we are the same as the animals, the same as the plants, and the same as the trees, and that all energy is matter and vice versa. This is a far cry from today's dominionists who believe superior humans own the earth and care not about how it is left after we're gone. The Buddha was clearly an environmentalist. He taught that if we destroy what is around us, we are destroying ourselves. And if we hurt another, we are hurting ourselves. He also taught that change is inevitable, much in keeping with the liberal willingness to change with the times.

Cause and effect, more succinctly known as karma, is another Buddhist teaching. We get what we deserve, and our thoughts and actions bring about our experiences. If you're a mean, liberal-hating mofo, those ill-feelings will only boomerang back to you. This is also true of mean, nasty conservative-hating mofos. To me, if you are a hater at all, even if you think you're a progressive, you are anything but liberal. I have incurred the wrath of liberals for working at a news organization that employs and appeals to conservatives. It would make some on the Left happy if, on occasion, I would haul off and clock one of them on national television. I've also been advised that if I were true to the liberal cause, I'd up and quit. Some of my fellow Lefties think they are doing their cause justice by never appearing on the Fox News Channel. I believe that this is a very non-liberal point of view. It is neither Jesus- nor Buddha-like. Neither of them preached only to the choir.

The most spiritually evolved minds are the ones truly in keeping with the teachings of not only Jesus but also the Buddha and Muhammad. These religious icons are not just the most spiritually evolved, they are also the most liberal—and they exemplify the values of every major religion in the United States, indeed in the world. These religions are the result of liberal thought, and they promote liberal ideas. They are based on kindness, compassion, and karma. The golden rule is so simple to explain yet so difficult to enact. Loving your neighbor sounds like a breeze until you actually try to do it. It's difficult enough to love our friends and even, often enough, our family; loving our enemies, for most of us, is out of the question.

The Unitarian Universalist Reverend Kimi Riegel summed up both liberalism and many of the world's religions when she wrote:

> To be a liberal, according to my favorite scripture, Merriam-Webster, is to be open-minded, is to be free from the constraints of dogmatism and authority, is to be generous and to believe in the basic goodness of humankind. Religion is defined as that which binds us back or reconnects us to that which is ultimately

important. Thus religious liberals are those that are connected, through generosity and openness, to the most important aspects of life. And therein lies the challenge. If we are open minded and not bound by authority who or what decides those matters of ultimate importance?

In that same sermon, she quoted the late Reverend William Sloane Coffin:

> On the religious side, liberals believe that the integrity of love is more important than the purity of dogma. Dogma is a sign post, love is a hitching post. Liberals contend that we should sharpen our minds, not narrow them. We understand that . . . faith, far from clearing up uncertainty, makes it possible to live with uncertainty. Fundamentalists, on the other hand, cannot bear uncertainty. They indulge in what psychiatrists call "premature closure" . . . Liberals contend that one of the most wonderful things about life is to act wholeheartedly without absolute certainty.

So there you have it. You may be angry at my argument; you may say that progressive policies have little to do with Christian values, or values of any of the world's religions. You may argue that liberal policies and actions strip personal responsibility, resulting in weak-willed people abandoning proper values. The true meaning of *freedom, liberty, patriotism,* and *being an American* may be in dispute, but how's this for an idea: Let's agree that both sides are correct. Freedom, or liberty, means the right to worship as we please, but also to marry who we love and to define our families as we see fit. Patriotism can be exhibited by a nice flag pin or by a "USA! USA!" shout-out at a political rally, but it can also be an inner feeling of love for our country that requires no lapel symbol or boisterous display.

The lyrics to "America the Beautiful," penned by Katherine Lee Bates, aren't just about "purple mountain majesties" and a "fruited plane." A bit further down, "alabaster cities gleam." The next time we sing these words that capture our national soul and make our chests fill with pride, let's remember how beautiful all of America is and the values we all share. Oh, and you might also be interested to know, as you belt out one of our most patriotic anthems, that the crafter of its words happened to be gay. *American* means all of the above. These are our liberal values. These are our American values.

A LITTLE HELP TO FIGHT THE RIGHT

The word *values* is not the province of the Right, but rather belongs to all of us, and that includes the often-heralded *family values* conservatives claim to own.

Words like *freedom, patriotism,* and even *American* can have different interpretations.

To a conservative, *freedom* can mean using government to enforce morality; to a liberal, it's protecting individual choices; and to a libertarian, it's no government at all.

Big flag pins and yelling "USA! USA!" at people with whom you disagree doesn't prove patriotism. Nor does voting for a "Patriot Act."

Contrary to Sarah Palin's statement, the entire country is part of "the pro-America areas" of America.

Ronald Reagan raised taxes 11 times, Bill Clinton left us with a surplus, and Barack Obama offered Republicans $2 trillion in spending cuts that they rejected, so stereotypes based on political ideology don't bear out.

Changing one's view when faced with new information and apologizing when you're wrong are good, American values.

Judaism, Islam, Buddhism, and Christianity are all based on liberal concepts.

All of us contribute to the values that make America great.

CHAPTER FIVE

WHO'S YOUR DEITY?

Nowhere does the left/right dichotomy play itself out more prominently than with the stark differences on those issues where religion is claimed as a policy determinant. Our First Amendment, beautifully crafted by our nation's founders, the very men conservatives claim to revere, addressed this from our beginnings. That's why religion and politics stayed in their respective corners for most of our history. But ever since Ronald Reagan made a political pact with what became the evangelical Right, this conflict has been bubbling under the surface, only to explode during the 2012 presidential race. Contraception, prenatal care, abortion, women's rights, and religious freedom to worship as we choose are areas you'd think were settled long ago. Acceptance in America of all religions—even those that are not expressly defined as Judeo-Christian, such as Islam, have always been at the very core of our patriotic DNA. Like Freddy Krueger, these issues keep coming back. It's Nightmare on Main Street.

But neither going back to bygone eras nor maintaining the status quo will do. In fact, maintaining the status quo is the same thing as going backward, for if you stand still, the world passes you by.

Liberals have the mission of saving us from the forces that would move us backward on key issues that affect all of us today. It's as though we must stop picking at long-ago healed wounds that create new scabs. The next time you're at a family dinner, and Uncle Charlie pontificates about how great it was the way things used to be, perhaps what is said here can help you puncture a few holes in his arguments.

People place their hand on the Bible and swear to uphold the Constitution. They don't put their hand on the Constitution and swear to uphold the Bible.
~Jamie Raskin

The concept of freedom of religion has been a cornerstone of America since our founding. Among the reasons we left merry ol' England, besides bad food and an odd accent, was the oppressiveness that comes when there is a state-sponsored church. At the time of the American Revolution, British government officials and professors had to take an oath to uphold the 39 articles of the Church of England. America's premise, and promise, was that church and state would not be intertwined and that the government should be religion-neutral. You wouldn't know that listening to a number of America's right-wing evangelicals, who believe that if you don't subscribe to their beliefs, you're going to hell. You wouldn't know that listening to conservatives railing against building a mosque in New York City, and you wouldn't know that listening to the field of 2012 presidential candidates who too often sound like they're vying for preacher-in-chief rather than commander-in-chief. Thankfully, American evangelicals have had little success codifying their religion into law, and the candidates conflating religion and politics aren't winning. But this doesn't mean that the general concept of separation of church and state isn't being constantly threatened by today's political environment, as is the entire concept of freedom of religion.

The notion that religious beliefs or lack thereof should not hold anyone back from any achievement, from being fully engaged in American life, or from being accepted as a full participant in our culture, is a bedrock tenet not only of our founders but also of liberalism itself. And it is liberals, to this day, who are the torch carriers ensuring that there is no religious test for public office and that your status as an American is not based on who your deity is. There is no attempt by liberals to impose religious beliefs on others, but rather an acknowledgment that we each find our own path. I'm sure the aforementioned right-wing evangelical Christians mean well when they tell me I'm going to Hell and that they're only trying to save me from a disastrous fate. They love Jews like me, if only because it's their belief that when the Rapture comes, we'll all accept the Lord Jesus. However, the idea of electing someone who thinks I'm going to Hell when my number is up makes me worry about what that politico would do for or to me while I'm still on the planet.

If you scratch the surface of religious legislators and candidates you find that their desires to impose restrictions on Americans are often biblically based. But government isn't supposed to tell us which sacred book to obey. In America we are supposed to be free to pick our own holy book and our own deity. Or none at all. Who or what you worship is none of my business and certainly not the business of our government. And who or what our office-seekers worship is also none of our business, so please, candidates, stop telling us how much you love God and Jesus and how much I'm supposed to in order to be considered a good American. When you do that you are making your religion my business, especially if you are in a position to make laws that affect my life.

Honestly, do we really care what religion our elected officials observe? The Constitution prohibits establishing any particular faith as the law of the land. Just as a reminder, the First Amendment (yes, the very first one, which means our beloved forefathers deemed it even more important than having guns) states: "Congress shall make no law respecting an establishment of religion . . ." Thus, it is known as the "Establishment Clause." Why should it be important to anyone what anyone else's faith is? Do they need to proselytize to convince others of their religious views because they're so insecure in them? Would knowing we all think alike religiously give them aid and comfort? God forbid we honor that dirty liberal word: diversity. (This is a good use of the word God, no?)

In 1960, John F. Kennedy gave a powerful speech to the Greater Houston Ministerial Association in which he outlined his views on the separation of church and state:

I believe in an America where the separation of church and state is absolute, where no Catholic prelate would tell the president (should he be Catholic) how to act, and no Protestant minister would tell his parishioners for whom to vote; where no church or church school is granted any public funds or political preference; and where no man is denied public office merely because his religion differs from the president who might appoint him or the people who might elect him.

I believe in an America that is officially neither Catholic, Protestant, nor Jewish; where no public official either requests or accepts instructions on public policy from the Pope, the National Council of Churches, or any other ecclesiastical source; where no religious body seeks to impose its will, directly or indirectly, upon the general populace or the public acts of its officials; and where religious liberty is so indivisible that an act against one church is treated as an act against all.

Presidential candidate Rick Santorum said that when he read these words, he "almost threw up." He originally said that in an October 2011 speech and then reasserted it on ABC's *This Week* in February 2012, in an interview with George Stephanopoulos. Santorum went way beyond revulsion with Kennedy, saying, "The idea that the church can have no influence or no involvement in the operation of the state is absolutely antithetical to the objectives and vision of our country." So here was a leading candidate for president, the victor of a number of Republican state primaries, who says the church should be involved in the operation of the state. Which church? If I'm a member of the Church of Satan can my church have a say? And in what way should a church be involved in "operating" a state? This part of Santorum's statement went largely ignored by the press. Where's "the liberal media" when you need it? And, ironically, had Kennedy not been so clear-minded about his own faith and its relationship to government, a Catholic like Rick Santorum might never have had the chance to run for president in the first place.

Because liberals are less guilty of mixing faith and policy, there is the impression that they are somehow less devoted to God. However, some of our most devout leaders have been liberals who didn't wear their religion on their sleeves, such as Jimmy Carter, former New York Governor Mario Cuomo, and most recently, President Barack Obama.

If you wanted a God-fearing Christian in office you couldn't have done better than Jimmy Carter. This son of a Southern Baptist preacher ultimately fell out with the Southern Baptist Convention. Actually, it was they who fell out with him when they refused to accept that Mormons are Christians. Carter eventually left the Southern Baptists altogether in 2000 when he couldn't abide by a denominational statement that women couldn't be pastors and that they were considered submissive to men. Carter was especially upset about the removal of an earlier statement that "the criterion by which the Bible is to be interpreted is Jesus Christ." The Georgia Democrat has been teaching Sunday School in Plains, Georgia, since he left the White House in 1981 and was among our most devout chief executives, but he never tried to push his own views on the rest of the country.

Former New York governor and practicing Catholic Mario Cuomo put it best when speaking at Notre Dame in 1984, explaining how he, much like John Kennedy, could honor the tenets of his faith without imposing it on his constituency:

> In addition to all the weaknesses, dilemmas, and temptations that impede every pilgrim's progress, the Catholic who holds political office in a pluralistic democracy—who is elected to serve Jews and Muslims, atheists and Protestants, as well as Catholics— bears special responsibility. He or she undertakes to help create conditions under which all can live with a maximum of dignity and with a reasonable degree of freedom; where everyone who chooses may hold beliefs different from specifically Catholic ones—sometimes contradictory to them; where the laws protect people's right to divorce, their right to use birth control, and even to choose abortion.
>
> In fact, Catholic public officials take an oath to preserve the Constitution that guarantees this freedom. And they do so gladly, not because they love what others do with their freedom but because they realize that in guaranteeing freedom for all, they guarantee our right to be Catholics: our right to pray, to use the sacraments, to refuse birth control devices, to reject abortion, not to divorce and remarry if we believe it to be wrong.
>
> The Catholic public official lives the political truth most Catholics through most of American history have accepted and insisted on: the truth that to assure our freedom we must allow others the same freedom, even if occasionally it produces conduct by them which we would hold to be sinful.
>
> I protect my right to be a Catholic by preserving your right to be a Jew, a Protestant, or a nonbeliever, or anything else you choose.

We know that the price of seeking to force our belief on others is that they might someday force theirs on us.

In June 2006 I had the opportunity to interview then-Senator Barack Obama after a speech he gave at the National Cathedral in Washington. Sponsored by Sojourners, it was titled the "Call to Renewal Address on Faith and Politics." With his typical eloquence, he offered one of the best explanations of how church and state can coexist:

> Democracy demands that the religiously motivated translate their concerns into universal, rather than religion-specific, values. It requires that their proposals be subject to argument and amenable to reason. I may be opposed to abortion for religious reasons, but if I seek to pass a law banning the practice, I cannot simply point to the teachings of my church or evoke God's will. I have to explain why abortion violates some principle that is accessible to people of all faiths, including those with no faith at all.
>
> Now this is going to be difficult for some who believe in the inerrancy of the Bible, as many evangelicals do. But in a pluralistic democracy, we have no choice. Politics depends on our ability to persuade each other of common aims based on a common reality. It involves the compromise, the art of what's possible. At some fundamental level, religion does not allow for compromise. It's the art of the impossible. If God has spoken, then followers are expected to live up to God's edicts, regardless of the consequences. To base one's life on such uncompromising commitments may be sublime, but to base our policy making on such commitments would be a dangerous thing.

John F. Kennedy, Jimmy Carter, Mario Cuomo, and Barack Obama were doing more than honoring their own faiths *while* not imposing them on others; they honored their faiths *by* not imposing them on others. By doing so, they honored the views of our forefathers and the very founding concepts of our nation. They understood where the line was between their own beliefs and their responsibility as public servants. Promoting their own religions in the name of public policy was not their job.

When religion and politics travel in the same cart, the riders believe nothing can stand in their way. Their movements become headlong—faster and faster and faster. They put aside all thoughts of obstacles and forget the precipice does not show itself to the man in a blind rush until it's too late. ~*Frank Herbert,* Dune

The 2012 presidential election became somewhat of a referendum on the line between church and state, particularly when Rick Santorum became the final "not Romney" and kept his focus on religiously influenced policy issues. While Santorum's strict religious views are to be respected, they are no business of ours, except that in his run for president, he made clear that his beliefs would be good guideposts for public policy. He even went so far as to say President Obama's policies were based on "some phony theology . . . not a theology based on the Bible." Perhaps we should remind him that our forefathers never meant for policy to be based on the Bible. But as Santorum has stated, his presidency would impose his own religious views. For example, he vowed that upon taking office, he would amend the constitution to state that marriage is between a man and a woman, thus nullifying all gay marriages that had been celebrated up to that point. Sadly this would also nullify our First Amendment.

Adding to his conflation of religion and policy, Santorum told an evangelical website in October 2011 that contraception was "not okay," and neither was sex for pleasure, for that matter:

> One of the things I will talk about that no president has talked about before, I think, is the dangers of contraception in this country, the whole sexual libertine idea. Many in the Christian faith have said, "Well, that's okay. Contraception's okay."
>
> It's not okay, because it's a license to do things in the sexual realm that is counter to how things are supposed to be. They're supposed to be within marriage, they are supposed to be for purposes that are, yes, conjugal, but also [inaudible], but also procreative. That's the perfect way that a sexual union should happen.

He concluded his comments by adding, "These are important public policy issues. These have profound impact on the health of our society."

I can't get that *Saturday Night Live* routine, "REALLY!?! With Seth and Amy," out of my head when I think about these comments. After each statement I want to say, "Really?" "Contraception is not okay." Really? "Consenting adults should not do things you don't like in the 'sexual realm.'" Really? "Sex is, at best, 'procreative.'" Really? "This should all be a matter of public policy." Really? What country is this, and what era? These conflicts are much more serious than the imagined "war on

Christmas" that liberals are theoretically waging, and it is up to progressives to save us from this madness.

Rick Santorum's rise as a presidential candidate also contributed to putting women in the crossfire. The 2012 Republican primaries coincided with implementation of part of the Affordable Care Act guaranteeing equal access to health care for all Americans, including access for women to contraceptive and prenatal coverage. The 769 Catholic hospitals that serve the general public employ people of all faiths—765,000 of them—and represent 14 percent of all hospital workers in the country. They are places of public accommodation, and they get tax dollars to boot. While the same law being put forth by the Affordable Care Act already existed in 28 states, 8 of which don't even exempt churches from the requirement to provide birth control care for women, no objection was raised until President Obama's health-care reforms were about to kick in. Even when the Obama administration went a step further to make sure that no religious institution had to bear the cost of this, transferring that responsibility to the insurance companies, the President and his supporters were accused of waging a war on religion. Given that 98 percent of Catholic women have used birth control and are permitted to do so by their church under a conscience clause, one has to wonder just where the war is really being waged and against whom. The Right attempted to make this about religious freedom, knowing that framing it that way would score them points with their base. But by making sure that women have access to prenatal care, which includes contraception, it is clearly really both a health and an equality issue, not a moral and religious one. No one objecting to providing birth control for women seemed to have a problem with Viagra for men. But then one provision prevents babies, and one is more likely to create them.

I will always be the virgin-prostitute, the perverse angel, the two-faced sinister and saintly woman.
~Anaïs Nin

The war on women isn't confined to the campaign trail. In spite of the President's compromise on shifting the burden of coverage from institutions to insurance companies, Republican Congressman Darrell Issa held a hearing on birth control and religious freedom, as if to prove that Democrats were taking that freedom away from good, religious Americans. No women were allowed to speak. Law student Sandra Fluke, past president of Georgetown University Law Students for Reproductive Justice, was poised and ready to go, but she was denied access to the witness table. Issa said Fluke was "not appropriate or qualified" to testify, even though she had worked as an advocate for unmarried victims of domestic violence and on the Manhattan Borough President's Taskforce on Domestic Violence. Three congresswomen walked out as a result. Fluke told me the night of the February 16, 2012, hearing, "I can't imagine who would be a more appropriate witness than someone speaking to assure the voices of the women who have been affected by the lack of contraceptive coverage and whose lives are going to be affected by this regulation." Fluke also made the point that contrary to the often-expressed view that contraception is cheap and affordable, it "can be a real financial burden for women. Contraception can cost $100 a month; that's $3,000 during law school. Three thousand dollars is the equivalent of what a public interest scholarship student like me makes during an entire summer, so it's not affordable." Furthermore, because of the economic recession, clinics providing vital services to women have been closing their doors or cutting hours as Congress and state legislatures have begun defunding them. Fluke relayed the story of a friend who suffered from polycystic ovary syndrome and needed contraception to prevent cysts from growing on her ovaries. Even though she was covered by Georgetown's medical plan, she was consistently denied her medical needs, which often happens, said Fluke, "because of a deep suspicion women are lying about their symptoms and that they really want this to prevent pregnancy." Fluke's friend wasn't seeking birth control for sex; she's gay. And her inability to procure her needed medication resulted in the loss of an ovary.

The threat to women's rights in America is real. A bill that passed the Arizona House and was endorsed by the Senate Judiciary Committee would have allowed an employer to fire a worker on the company health plan for using birth control to prevent pregnancy if the employer found it morally objectionable. This would force women receiving contraception through work to reveal medical conditions to their bosses or risk losing their jobs if the employer found out. This is not about religious freedom as conservatives claim; it's about forcing an employer's views on others, with the "others" being women. The bill's sponsor, Republican Debbie Lesko, is by all accounts, and unfathomably, a woman.

**We really need to get over this love affair with
the fetus and start worrying about children.**
~Joycelyn Elders

The wars on birth control, health care, and women are intertwined and are being waged on many fronts. A similar effort to take us back to prehistoric times, or at least pre-women's movement times, is the push in state legislatures to pass "personhood laws." This is a sneaky way to creep toward outlawing abortion. If they can legally declare a zygote a human being, they can then define abortion—and the birth control pill—as murder. Initiative 26 in Mississippi failed in November 2011, and the Virginia and Georgia legislatures put similar laws on ice in 2012, knowing they were too controversial for a major election year. In Oklahoma, a strong backlash to such legislation resulted in women leaving their shoes on the steps of the state Capitol, insinuating that conservative legislators wanted them barefoot and pregnant. Democratic Senator Judy Eason McIntyre held up a sign saying, "If I wanted the government in my womb, I'd f--- a senator." I've substituted dashes for letters in that sign, just in case Big Brother is watching. Frankly, if zygotes are human beings, what do we do for them next? Make sure fertilized eggs can all have guns? It would be wonderful if some on the Right loved the poor, the sick, and the elderly as much as they love fetuses.

Another sneaky way of approaching the abortion issue is requiring women to have sonograms before allowing them to have abortions. In Texas, a doctor has to meet with a woman seeking an abortion at least 24 hours ahead of time to administer a sonogram, describe abortion risks, and determine the gestational age of the fetus. The abortion provider has to show the woman images from the sonogram, make the heartbeat audible, and describe the fetus. A woman can opt out of listening to the description only if she certifies in writing that she was sexually assaulted, a victim of incest, or that the fetus has an irreversible medical condition. Should we really be asking women to have to provide notes like schoolchildren asking to be excused from class in order to exercise their rights?

Virginia and Alabama were close to enacting laws requiring women to have invasive ultrasounds where transducers, or wands, would be inserted into their vaginas before they could consent to abortions. The Alabama bill was rewritten so women could choose either the vaginal ultrasound or the less invasive abdominal one. Virginia Governor Bob McDonnell was about to sign a similar bill until his attorney general told him that mandating such an invasive procedure was a Fourth Amendment violation. It's a bummer when that pesky Constitution gets in the way, isn't it? As in Alabama, the law was changed to provide a choice between transvaginal and transabdominal ultrasounds. This is their version of being pro-choice.

Some innovative liberal state legislators fought fire with fire and beautifully made their points in the process. Ohio State Senator Nina Turner was becoming disgusted watching men pass restrictive laws about women's reproductive health. "We should show the same attention and love to men's reproductive health as we do to women's," she stated. And so she offered up a bill to require men to get psychological counseling to verify they had medical reasons to get prescriptions for erectile dysfunction drugs like Viagra. And doctors would be required to inform men in writing of the risks of taking such drugs.

Oklahoma State Senator Constance Johnson sponsored a "spilled-semen amendment" to her state's personhood bill to make it a crime against unborn children to waste sperm. In Illinois, State Representative Kelly Cassidy wanted an amendment to the state's ultrasound bill to require men to watch a video warning about Viagra's side effects before they could enjoy the fruits of that sexual enhancer. And City Councilwoman Loretta Walsh in Wilmington, Delaware, wrote a resolution declaring "each 'egg person' and each 'sperm person' should be deemed equal in the eyes of the government." The Family Research Council's Jeanne Monahan, who runs their Center for Human Dignity, sniffed, "It sounds like they're mocking pro-life bills." Yup. That's what they're doing all right. Hurts when that shoe is on the other foot, doesn't it?

Note that the legislators standing up to misogynistic laws are women—and Democrats. Perhaps we should elect more people who can speak about women's issues from a firsthand point of view. Men, if you don't think a woman should have the right to choose what to do with her reproductive organs, sorry, those organs don't belong to you, so you may not have standing to legislate or rule on them.

In the practice of tolerance, one's enemy is the best teacher. ~*The Dalai Lama*

While the religious Right and the politicians who love them (when it's convenient) have bellowed that President Obama and liberals are conspiring to squelch religious freedom, the lack of tolerance they have exhibited shows this to be a classic case of projection. Since

9/11, we've seen an erosion of much of the religious tolerance that's been fought for over the years. As I said before, America was founded on the belief that your religion or lack thereof should not hold you back from any achievement or from being accepted as a full participant in our society. Your status as an American is not based on who your deity is. Sadly, the post-9/11 era has brought that concept screeching to a halt.

The New York City Police Department used 9/11 as an excuse for secret surveillance of Muslims, according to documents unearthed by the Associated Press in February 2012. Revealed was a 2006 plan to monitor neighborhoods and spy on mosques. The NYPD was already under fire for using an anti-Muslim documentary, *The Third Jihad,* as a training film. The AP also discovered that the department assigned undercover officers called "rakers" to infiltrate minority neighborhoods and watch bookstores, bars, cafes, and nightclubs, and it also used informants known as "mosque crawlers." New York's Police Commissioner, Raymond Kelly, defended this as necessary "to protect everyone." Big Brother would be proud. Just like the Patriot Act and George Orwell's Ministry of Truth, it is exactly the opposite of the words being used.

Presidential candidate Herman Cain said he wouldn't put a Muslim in his cabinet because of a "creeping attempt . . . to gradually ease Sharia law and the Muslim faith into our government." He then amended his position saying Mormons would be acceptable as long as they took loyalty tests, proclaiming, "That's not discrimination. It's called trying to protect the American people. This nation is under attack constantly by people who want to kill all of us, so I'm going to take extra precaution." Then Cain denied to Matthew Wells of the BBC that he ever said he wouldn't put a Muslim in his cabinet. And he told Chris Wallace on *Fox News Sunday* that communities should be able to ban mosques and denied it was religious discrimination.

It's laughable that conservatives accused President Obama of infringing on religious liberty by expanding women's health care, and yet this same group displayed bigotry toward Muslims that would never be tolerated if it were directed at conservative Christians. Rick Santorum whined that progressives "are taking faith and crushing it . . . when you marginalize faith in America . . . what's left is the French Revolution." Santorum wagged his finger in the air and warned, "What's left is the guillotine . . . If we follow the path of President Obama and his overt hostility to faith in America . . . then we are headed down that road." Campaigning in Florida in January 2011, Newt Gingrich referred to "the Obama administration's attack on Christianity . . . a fundamental assault on the right of freedom of religion." He vowed that, "on the very first day I'm inaugurated, I will sign an executive order repealing every Obama attack on religion across the entire government, period." He added, "I think we need to have a government that respects our religion. I'm a little bit tired of being lectured about respecting every other religion on the planet." Wait a minute! I didn't know there was an "our religion," nor did I realize that America was set up with an us-versus-them dichotomy in religious preference, with a hierarchy of respect levels. Similarly, Mitt Romney claimed President Obama has "fought against religion." But look who's fighting religion when it comes to the right of a church to build a prayer center.

When the so-called Ground Zero mosque was being considered for a space in lower Manhattan, Newt Gingrich said, "America is experiencing an Islamist cultural-political offensive designed to undermine and destroy our civilization." Candidate Romney opined that "the potential for extremists to use the mosque for global recruiting and propaganda compel[s] rejection of this site." Since when, in America, do we tell those who wish to pray as they please that setting up a place to do so makes them global recruiters and propagandists? Are Christians the only ones allowed to recruit for their faith?

New York City Mayor Michael Bloomberg offered up his finest hour when he went to Governors Island with City Council Speaker Christine Quinn and spoke on behalf of the mosque and for religious freedom. They chose Governors Island, he said, because it's "where the earliest settlers first set foot in New Amsterdam, and where the seeds of religious tolerance were first planted." The mayor reminded the world that he helms a city "sustained by immigrants, by people from more than 100 different countries speaking more than 200 different languages and professing every faith. And whether your parents were born here or you came here yesterday, you are a New Yorker." And an American, by the way. Given the level of anti-Muslim rhetoric and bigotry flying around, it took moxie for the mayor to add: "Muslims are as much a part of our city and our country as the people of any faith, and they are as welcome to worship in lower Manhattan as any other group. In fact, they have been worshipping at the site for the better part of a year, as is their right. The local community board in lower Manhattan voted overwhelmingly to support the proposal, and if it moves forward, I expect the community center and mosque will add to the life and vitality of the neighborhood and the entire city."

Too many Americans have decided to judge an entire religion by the actions of a few who don't properly represent the Islamic faith. We don't judge all Christians by those few who kill abortion doctors in the name of Jesus, and we shouldn't be judgmental of others who bastardize any other religion to advance their own sick agendas. Liberals need to call out those whose illiberal words and actions are hurting America—just as Bloomberg and Quinn did.

Strangely, this "Ground Zero mosque" wasn't even at Ground Zero, and it wasn't just a mosque but rather an intercultural educational center. Yet the term *Ground Zero mosque* stuck, as those who oppose Islam believed such a structure shouldn't exist anywhere near what they view as hallowed ground. What many of them truly believe is that mosques don't belong anywhere in America. The Park51 Islamic Center, which is modeled on the YMCA, not a terrorist training camp, finally opened to little fanfare. If, as its detractors believe, it is anathema to have a place of worship for Muslims two blocks from the site of the World Trade Center, how far is acceptable? Four blocks? Ten blocks? Who, exactly, is to decide? It reminds me of the comedian Robert Klein's description of his father as the guy on the beach who is the self-appointed arbiter of when you can go back in the water after a meal:

"What did you have? A tuna sandwich? With a pickle?"

"Yes."

"Thirty-three minutes. Peanut butter and jelly? Twenty-seven minutes. Bologna and cheese? Forty-two minutes. Frankfurters and beans? Too heavy. You can't go swimming this year."

"How far is the mosque from Ground Zero? Two blocks?"

"Yes."

"Unacceptable; that's a victory mosque. Four blocks? The terrorists win. Anywhere in New York City? Too close for comfort. The closest it can be: Afghanistan."

The bigots didn't want the Islamic center anywhere, any year. Frankly, they ought to be more concerned about their own salvation than imposing their views on a society that doesn't need and shouldn't welcome their pronouncements.

Pamela Geller, the prime mover against the presence of the Park51 Islamic Center, said it was typical of Muslims to "build triumphal mosques on the cherished sites of sacred lands of conquered lands." Really? I didn't realize that lower Manhattan is now occupied by a foreign power. Geller also referred to Park51 as a "kick in the head" and a stab in the eye to Americans, and "the second wave of the 9/11 attacks."

When pictures surfaced of Marines urinating on corpses of freshly killed Taliban soldiers, "the queen of the Muslim bashers," as Geller is sometimes called, proclaimed, "I love these Marines." Muslim tradition is that the body of the deceased is washed before burial, however not quite the way the Marines did it. The Obama administration honored this practice and showed our religious tolerance as a nation when bin Laden was captured and killed. They made sure that his body was bathed and wrapped according to Islamic custom and buried within 24 hours of death. This predictably upset conservative Americans, who didn't believe the body of the world's best-known terrorist deserved any consideration. However, upholding religious tradition, even for our most ardent enemy, is what we should expect of a country built on religious freedom. We don't live by the standards of our enemy. When Korans were incinerated in a burn pit at the Bagram base in Afghanistan leading to riots, President Obama again exhibited American ideals when he sent a letter of apology to Afghan president Hamid Karzai, again incurring the wrath of the Right. But the statement of regret, besides being proper, was to protect our own soldiers from a citizenry enraged by our actions.

Unfortunately, intolerance toward Muslims is widespread and is fed by those who promote fear and ignorance. Anti-Muslim activist John Joseph Jay called for the murder of Muslims (along with gays, liberals, and journalists) and said mosques should be burned to the ground. Jihad Watch's Robert Spencer called for a boycott of Campbell's Soup for making broth that is halal-certified. Can you imagine calling for a boycott of companies that make foods kosher for Passover?

Former Reagan official Frank Gaffney objected to the appointment of Elena Kagan to the Supreme Court believing she was sympathetic to Sharia law, and when *The Washington Times* published his op-ed on the issue, they phonied-up a picture of the then-nominee with a turban on her head. Gaffney also went on a mission to change the logo of the Missile Defense Agency because he thought it looked too much like the Star and Crescent, which he also claimed looked like the Obama logo. (Get it? He's a secret Muslim!)

Christians should not forget that the kind of bigotry now directed at Muslims is not unlike the prejudice Catholics faced in the 19th century, when want ads often contained the words "Irish need not apply," which was code for anti-Catholic sentiment. But I believe that the day will come in America when people of all faiths will enjoy acceptance. Liberals have fought and will continue to fight for this religious tolerance. It took liberals to give us our first Catholic president. It took liberals to give us our first Jewish vice presidential candidate. And liberals broke the glass ceiling of Muslims in Congress when Andre Carson of Indiana and Keith Ellison of Minnesota made it to Washington only within the last few years. As the first Muslim to be elected to Congress, Ellison had to endure taunts from alarmed conservatives that his swearing-in would take place on the Koran. This is false, if only because swearings-in are not done using religious texts, although pictures were taken after the ceremony with Ellison holding the holy book. But even though Ellison did have a Koran in hand after his induction, you can look around and see that the republic still stands.

Ellison has had to endure many other indignities because of his faith. Tea Party Nation sent out mailers supporting his 2010 opponent, Lynne Torgerson, using scare tactics against Ellison, claiming, "He has a ZERO rating from the American Conservative Union. He is the only Muslim member of Congress. He supports the Council on American-Islamic Relations [and] Hamas, and has helped Congress send millions of tax [dollars] to terrorists in Gaza."

An anti-Muslim group petitioned Democratic Congressman Ron Klein of Fort Lauderdale, Florida, to remove Ellison from an anti-Semitism task force, screeching, "We demand that he does so immediately. Every day that Ellison sits on that task force is an offense to those who fell victim to anti-Semitism and/or radical Islam."

To his credit, Klein refused to take that bait. The name of the group that went after Ellison: "Americans Against Hate." How funny is that? That would be like calling the birthers "The Obama Appreciation Society."

No wonder Ellison teared up when he spoke at Long Island Congressman Peter King's congressional hearings on the so-called radicalization of Muslims. Ellison told the story of Mohammed Salman Hamdani, a Muslim first responder who died on 9/11 rescuing people from the World Trade Center. Hamdani's allegiance had been questioned simply because of his faith. Ellison tearfully relayed:

> Mr. Hamdani bravely sacrificed his life to try and help others on 9/11. After the tragedy some people tried to smear his character solely because of his Islamic faith. Some people spread false rumors and speculated that he was in league with the attackers only because he was Muslim. It was only when his remains were identified that these lies were fully exposed. Mohammed Salman Hamdani was a fellow American who gave his life for other Americans. His life should not be defined as a member of an ethnic group or a member of a religion but as an American who gave everything for his fellow citizens.

Let us never forget that Muslims died on 9/11, rescued people on 9/11, and fought in our post–9/11 wars. And these wars were fought in Muslim countries where thousands of Americans gave their lives, and thousands more gave their limbs and other body parts so that Muslims could have freer and more democratic lives.

Congressman King sat stone-faced as Ellison gave this emotional testimony. King is the same congressman who once said, there are "too many mosques in this country . . . There are too many people sympathetic to radical Islam. We should be looking at them more carefully and finding out how we can infiltrate them." King later claimed he never said that, even though it's a matter of record. King's revised version was that he said there are "too many mosques that don't cooperate with law enforcement . . . I never said there were too many mosques in America." Someone needs to inform Representative King about the existence of YouTube.

King's hearings were a 2000s version of the House Un-American Activities Committee, a one-sided anti-Muslim slugfest. After claiming he would have a range of law enforcement officials giving various views of their relationships with Muslims, only one official was called, and that invitation came from Democrats. Los Angeles Sheriff Lee Baca offered actual statistics: "Since 9/11, 77 extremist efforts or attacks have been carried out by non-Muslim extremists in the United States." In addition, of the last 10 terror plots attempted by Muslims, 7 of them have been thwarted by Muslims coming forward. As Baca explained, "This is not a Muslim problem; it's a people problem."

Ironically, Peter King himself was considered a threat in 1984, when Ronald Reagan was visiting King's native Nassau County, because of King's allegiance with the Irish Republican Army, then considered a terrorist group. Of course, one person's terrorist is another's freedom fighter. It's a shame he and those who support his inquests ignore the very real facts about Muslims in the United States.

University of North Carolina sociology professor Charles Kurzman authored a study, "Muslim-American Terrorism in the Decade Since 9/11," released in February 2012, containing numbers that defy much of the general attitude about Muslims and Islam. For example, the number of Muslim Americans who committed, or were arrested for, terrorist crimes in 2011: 20. That's down from 26 in 2010 and 49 in 2009. Interestingly, these offenders don't match any ethnic or racial profile. Their makeup is 30 percent Arab, 25 percent white, and 15 percent African American—percentages that are no different from those in prior years. He also laid out the number of Muslim Americans arrested for or convicted of violent terrorism acts since 9/11: 193.

In terms of the threat to public safety, compare these numbers to the 14,000 murders that took place in the United States in 2011, most of which probably had nothing to do with Islamic extremism.

Most notable is that a large number of tips to law enforcement alerting them to potential terrorist plots are from Muslim Americans. Of the 140 initial tips that could be verified since 9/11, 52 came from Muslim Americans. Peter King and those like him who are suspicious of Muslims in America ought to be congratulating them rather than investigating them.

Do you know who has a laudable record of Muslim outreach? George W. Bush. Bush referred to Islam as "a noble faith" and said the religion offers "hope and comfort." Bush is on record as having said many times, both in the wake of 9/11 and for years afterward, that Islam is not our enemy. Unlike some of his conservative brethren, Bush never came across as an intolerant bigot.

The late author and essayist C.S. Lewis said, "We all want progress. But . . . if you're on the wrong road, progress means doing an about-turn and walking back to the right road; and in that case, the man who turns back soonest is the most progressive. . ." When I speak of liberals saving America, it involves not just advocating for good public policy, for justice, for peace, for women's rights, and for religious freedom. It's not as simple as just moving forward. We have to get off the wrong road and stop litigating long-ago, hard-won battles. We must also stand guard against those who would impose their own privately held views on the rest of us. Lord knows (okay, make that "Deity or lack thereof knows") where they would take the country if the reins were off.

A LITTLE HELP TO FIGHT THE RIGHT

Politics married religion with Ronald Reagan conducting the ceremony in 1980, and that hasn't been good for either. We left merry ol' England hoping this marriage would never take place.

A politician's religious views only matter when they try to make them matters of public policy.

Rick Santorum said JFK's speech on keeping his faith out of politics made him want to throw up. Santorum's efforts to put his faith into politics have a similar nauseating effect on progressives.

Liberals not mixing faith with politics doesn't mean they're less devout. Contrary to stereotypes, some of our most religious leaders, like Mario Cuomo, Jimmy Carter, and Barack Obama have been on the Left.

Insisting that insurance companies that service Catholic-run institutions (not the church itself) provide reproductive care to women is not a war on religion. Denying care, however, is a war on women.

Requiring women to have sonograms, listen to fetal heartbeats, and observe waiting periods before abortions are sneaky ways of trying to stop women's freedom of choice.

Some of the same people accusing President Obama of conducting a war on religion support spying on Muslims, preventing the building of mosques, and worry that America will be subject to Sharia law.

Muslims died on 9/11, worked as first responders, and fight in our military, often protecting Muslim countries.

Who your deity is, or having none at all, has no bearing on being an American.

CHAPTER SIX

AMERICA HAS ISSUES

Adding to what C.S. Lewis said, once we're on the right road, there's a reason to stay in the left lane. Is it any wonder that the left lane moves faster than the right one does? Let's face it: America has issues, and they're pressing ones. We are not doing all we can to protect the most vulnerable members of society: caring for the poor; providing for the immigrants who come here to do work we won't and don't do; or providing drug users with treatment, not jail time. We also fail to protect the environment as we should, or even our own well-being, involving ourselves in unnecessary wars that make us more vulnerable to attack. We have issues, and when it comes to tackling them, left is right and right is wrong.

[A] Corporation . . . may not commit treason, nor be outlawed, nor excommunicate, for they have no souls, neither can they appear in person, but by Attorney.
~Sir Edward Coke

Let's begin here with the fundamental question about just what constitutes a person. The Citizens United ruling put electioneering by corporations on the same footing as electioneering by individuals, thus equating corporations with people. But you wouldn't say that a corporation, unlike a government, is, in the words of Abraham Lincoln, "of the people, by the people, for the people." And that is the problem with Citizens United. In this case, conservative jurist Antonin Scalia agreed with the conservative majority that the text of the First Amendment "offers no foothold for excluding any category of speaker." In other words, a corporation has the same rights as a person. This seems wrong. I don't believe we can trust in the inherent kindness and goodness of corporations, which are ruled by the profit motive, to always do the right thing. Remember Enron?

But this distinction didn't faze Mitt Romney. During a campaign event, when he was talking about taxes and the idea of corporations paying their fair share, Romney declared, "Corporations are people, my friend." "No they're not," someone up front yelled back, to which Romney answered, "Of course they are. Everything corporations earn ultimately goes to people. Where do you think it goes?" Well, if you own stock in a company and the company declares a dividend, that may be the case, but not everyone is so fortunate. So, sure, I guess you could say that corporations are people, but let's face it, if they are, they're wealthy people. They don't accurately represent the lower-level workers who make them run.

They are not the workers, who don't benefit from dividends paid. The concern of a corporation is the bottom line, which doesn't necessarily include regard for the greater good. Perhaps Romney's inability to see this distinction is why he has such a hard time relating to the average voter.

It's true that people together form corporations, which are bigger, nonpersonal entities that don't always act in the interest of individuals or promote their rights. The Constitution applies to "persons," which is why I believe Scalia and his conservative brethren got it wrong. The rights of people can and often should be applied to corporations, such as the right to sue or be sued. The United States Code even states that for "any Act of Congress, unless the context indicates otherwise . . . the words 'person' and 'whoever' include corporations . . ." However, it is impractical and even silly to expect that a corporation can be considered an individual in every circumstance. Corporations don't have the right to go into the voting booth to choose our representatives and presidents, but I bet many conservatives wish they did. If they did have that right, they would also have to live by other regulations that apply to those who are undeniably people. Would corporations have to be 18 years old before they could vote? Can a corporation claim it has the right to own a gun? Can a corporation serve on a jury? If you go through life equating a person with a corporation, you're going to have some awkward moments.

You: Table for two, please.

Maître d': Yes, Mr. Colmes, and who will be joining you?

You: The Bank of America.

Setting a precedent that a corporation is a person has far-ranging consequences. For example, a Sixth Circuit federal judge ruled in March 2012 to stop the Food and Drug Administration from requiring tobacco companies to put graphic warning labels on tobacco products, siding with tobacco companies that this was a free-speech violation. This decision goes against what should be the role of government—to provide a level playing ground for all citizens, not for all corporations.

Efforts are underway by progressive groups and legislators to overturn the Citizens United decision. Some Californians are promoting the Corporations Are Not People Act, which would "affirm that only human beings are people entitled to the constitutional rights of a person in California." California Assemblymembers Bob Wieckowski and Michael Allen introduced a resolution calling for Congress to introduce a constitutional amendment establishing that corporations are not people; legislatures in New Mexico, Hawaii, and Vermont have already passed such resolutions. In Arcata, California, residents gathered signatures for a "Corps Ain't People" initiative. Two dozen Congressmen led by Jim McGovern of Massachusetts have cosponsored the People's Rights Amendment, asserting that the words *people* and *person* in the Constitution apply only to actual human beings. This sounds as though it would be in keeping with what conservatives say they favor when interpreting the Constitution: "original intent."

Whatever you did for the least of my brothers and sisters, you did for Me. ~*Matthew 25:40*

The Liberals' desire for an even playing field demands that we fight for the rights and well-being of all, regardless of race, creed, religion, or gender. This often means that we stand up for those who are least able to do so for themselves. For years, there seems to have been a battle being waged against the poor, from attempts at cutting welfare benefits to restricting voting rights to infringing on the basic human rights and dignity of immigrants. And it's been liberals who have stood up and fought in each of these situations.

President Obama's stimulus package not only saved the country from a steep economic decline, it also targeted the needs of poverty-stricken Americans. The American Recovery and Reinvestment Act added $20 billion to the food-stamp program, provided $1.5 billion in homelessness prevention funds to enable people to either stay in their homes or quickly find new housing, provided money for job training, and increased unemployment benefits by $25 a week per recipient. As America began to recover from the worst economy since the Great Depression, it was Democrats in the House and Senate who fought to reauthorize unemployment benefits so that needy Americans could be covered for up to 99 weeks. After much wrangling at the end of 2011, Democrats took the lead to pass the Middle Class Tax Relief and Job Creation Act of 2012, which again extended benefits for those who hadn't yet recovered from years of financial hardships.

Because of moves like this and because of the high rate of unemployment during President Obama's term, Newt Gingrich referred to Barack Obama as "the food-stamp president" in the heat of the 2012 presidential race, noting that the number of food-stamp recipients was at an all-time high. But he also claimed that Obama "put" more people on food stamps than any other president, which is untrue. At the time Gingrich made this statement, 14.2 million Americans had entered the program under Obama, compared to 14.7 million during the George W. Bush administration. Interestingly, the food-stamp program became the vehicle to help needy families because of the very welfare reform promoted by a former congressman named . . . wait for it . . . Newt Gingrich. Does that make him the "food-stamp Speaker"? The 1996 changes in welfare reform he helped initiate provided for expanding the food-stamp program (SNAP) during tough economic times. Dare we add Newt Gingrich, like Ronald Reagan before him, to the list of big government liberals?

And liberal efforts don't only come from the government. Grassroots efforts do much to address societal ills. LIFT, which was founded by Kirsten Lodal in 1998 when she was a Yale sophomore, is one example. Lodal recognized that working parents with low-wage jobs still couldn't sustain their families and needed help connecting to social services and each other to survive. Lodal, like many liberals, knows that not everyone has a built-in support system of family, friends, religious community, or mentors. LIFT has helped 40,000 families out of poverty and, as of 2012, works with 6,000 clients to help them get jobs, education, and training, and find safe and affordable housing.

The liberal push—both governmental and individual—to help those who'd temporarily fallen on hard times began to pay off. By April 2012, claims for unemployment benefits hit a four-year low.

Unfortunately, these efforts occurred alongside conservative pushes in the other direction. If you're poor, picking yourself up and dusting yourself off has become much tougher for residents of Republican-led states. In

June 2011, Florida Governor Rick Scott announced with great fanfare that his state's welfare recipients would be required to submit to drug testing, promising that this would save the state money. And the poor, the very ones seeking assistance, were required to pay for blood, urine, and hair samples before they could receive cash benefits. What a coincidence that Solantic, the company Scott founded, realized much of its profits from the business of drug testing. Not only was this drug-testing mandate ruled illegal by a federal judge under the Fourth Amendment, as it is considered an illegal search, but it actually cost the state money. Ninety-six percent of those tested were drug free, and the state had to reimburse them for the costs of the testing. Florida ought to thank the ACLU, which brought the suit to stop this practice, for providing the savings the state will realize and for eliminating bureaucracy they won't need. The argument that the needy take drugs out of proportion to the rest of the population was disproven in Florida. The 2009 National Survey on Drug Use and Health showed that 8.7 percent of the entire U.S. population over age 12 uses drugs, far above the 2 percent of Floridians who were users when they applied for assistance.

Florida Republicans even went so far as attempting to legislate away the ability of food-stamp users to buy snacks. This would have prevented a mother from even buying her child a birthday cake. I regularly get calls on my radio show from angry taxpayers who believe that food-stamp recipients are lazy bums who just want to gobble up the hard-earned tax dollars of hard-working Americans. When these social misfits aren't sitting in front of the television feasting on the beer and Ring Dings they bought with government handouts, they're busy having indiscriminate sex so they can get pregnant, have more babies, and thus get more government dollars. Or so their detractors would have you believe.

For those who need a helping hand, it's awfully severe to deny them the occasional beer or cupcake. It's not as if they're scarfing down beluga caviar with what little resources they have. Furthermore, according to a 2008 Moody's study, for every dollar spent with food stamps, there is $1.73 of economic activity. (The Department of Agriculture puts the figure at $1.76.) For every dollar of unemployment benefits, the return is $1.64. An average family of four gets approximately $500 worth of food stamps a month and can receive $900 from the Temporary Assistance for Needy Families program. These numbers don't exactly allow you to live high on the hog. The notion that women are baby-making schemers turning their uteruses into money-minting conveyer belts defies logic. It also insults women.

I don't know about you, but I'm motivated to work, and on those occasions when an employer wised up and let me go, I was motivated to find new work. You're likely the same way. So why should we believe that other Americans are any different, just because they may have fallen on hard times? Aren't we all part of the same American family? The notion that folks don't want to work is disproven by job fairs around the country that are attracting thousands of people. The United Jewish Appeal of New York Connect to Care program had job fairs in the first two months of 2011 that drew 36,000 people. In August 2011, Chicago State University conducted a transportation job fair that had almost 10,000 attendees. I doubt they were just getting out of the house because they were bored and *Jeopardy!* was in reruns.

I am sure that every one of my colleagues—Democrat, Republican, and Independent—agrees . . . [t]hat in the voting booth, everyone is equal. *~Barbara Boxer*

While it's true that everyone is equal in the voting booth, sometimes the problem lies in getting to that voting booth in the first place. Paul Weyrich, the late co-founder of both the Heritage Foundation, a conservative think tank, and the Moral Majority, and considered the "father" of the conservative movement, had this to say while addressing evangelicals in 1980:

> Now many of our Christians have what I call the goo-goo syndrome—good government. They want everybody to vote. I don't want everybody to vote. Elections are not won by a majority of people; they never have been from the beginning of our country, and they are not now. As a matter of fact, our leverage in the elections quite candidly goes up as the voting populace goes down.

Aha! There you have it: a bold admission that right-wing election success rests on keeping people out of the voting booth. And the people who are kept out happen to be the least privileged of our society.

NYU's Brennan Center for Justice estimated that an array of laws put in place by Republican legislatures for the 2012 election make it tougher to vote for more than 5 million Americans—more than the margin of victory in two of the last three presidential elections. Some states ended early voting; others reversed laws that allowed criminals who had paid their debt to society to vote. The changes affect mostly the young, the poor, minorities, and voters with disabilities. Laws making it more difficult for voters to identify themselves especially hurt minorities and the poor.

In 2002, the Bush administration pushed and got passed the Help America Vote Act, which required any voter registering by mail who had never before voted in a federal election to show a valid ID. It is well known that those in the country a short time, as well as the poor and the elderly, are less likely to have proper identification and that blacks and Hispanics are also hurt by these rules.

While it is argued that these laws are being put in place to stem voter fraud—making America a truer democracy—it seems hard to believe. To paraphrase Mark Twain, evidence of voter fraud has been greatly exaggerated. Indiana has the strictest photo-ID law in the nation, and a conservative Supreme Court upheld it in 2008, even though no one has been prosecuted for voter-ID fraud in that state. The Election Assistance Commission studied a five-year crackdown on voter fraud by the Bush 43 administration between 2002 and 2007 and found out there was very little of it. Republicans in Florida, New Mexico, Pennsylvania, and Washington made a push to have stricter voting laws, and there was particular interest in the swing states of Wisconsin and Ohio; but there weren't many cases of voter fraud, and most accusations resulted in acquittals. In Wisconsin, every case of double voting was decided in favor of the defendant. Out of hundreds of suspected violations in Milwaukee, only 14, mostly black and poor voters, ever faced federal charges. Funny that almost all of those accused were Democrats. Election law expert Richard L. Hasen of Loyola Law says, "If they found a single case of a conspiracy to affect the outcome of a Congressional election or a statewide election, that would be significant. But what we see [are] isolated, small-scale activities that often have not shown any kind of criminal intent." In spite of this, the Bush administration removed two U.S. attorneys who were accused of not pursuing cases.

In 2011, eyeing the upcoming presidential election, more than a dozen states passed stricter voting laws. Republican governors in Pennsylvania, Ohio, Wisconsin, and Texas were particularly aggressive. Rick Perry of Texas made it an "emergency item." Funny that in that state, a gun permit is considered valid identification, but a college ID isn't, again showing that the push for these laws is meant to favor Republicans and keep Democrats away from the polls.

Galloping to the rescue were both liberal groups and the Obama administration. In March 2012, the Department of Justice stepped in to block the Texas voter ID law. In Wisconsin, liberal groups such as the ACLU and a civil rights think tank called the Advancement Project are challenging the voter-ID law in federal court. The ACLU claims it violates the Equal Protection Clause of the Fourteenth Amendment, and the Advancement Project challenge is based on a possible violation of the Voting Rights Act. As a result, Wisconsin Circuit Judge Richard G. Niess denied a request by the state government to enforce the law ahead of that state's April 3 primary. Niess wrote, "An unconstitutional law is void ab initio." That's one of those Latin legal terms which the judge went on to explain: "It is as if it never existed. Therefore there can be no justification for enforcement." A second court refused to enact Wisconsin's restrictive voter-ID law ahead of the state's recall election. In Pennsylvania, Democrats regard Republican Governor Tom

Corbett's signing of a voter-ID bill as a way to reduce the number of Democrats likely to vote for President Obama in the 2012 election. The County Commissioners Association says there are already preventive systems in place to stop false ballots, and the new law will create confusion but with no added ballot security. The NAACP, labor unions, and the AARP are outspoken critics of this unnecessary and restrictive law.

In December 2011, the Justice Department blocked a South Carolina law requiring a photo ID to vote. Assistant Attorney General for Civil Rights Thomas Perez wrote:

> In sum, however analyzed, the state's data demonstrate that non-white voters are both significantly burdened by section 5 of Act R54 in absolute terms, and also disproportionately unlikely to possess the most common types of photo identification among the forms of identification that would be necessary for in-person voting under the proposed law.
>
> . . . Until South Carolina succeeds in substantially addressing the racial disparities described above, however, the state cannot meet its burden of proving that, when compared to the benchmark standard, the voter identification requirements proposed in section 5 of Act R54 will not have a retrogressive effect . . . .

Perez also stated there was no evidence of voter fraud in South Carolina in the first place that would require this kind of more restrictive law.

While these laws were created to deal with a problem that doesn't exist, they affect real people who do, like Dorothy Cooper, a 96-year-old retired domestic worker who was born before women had the right to vote. She was denied an ID in Tennessee because she couldn't produce her marriage certificate. Her birth certificate was no good because it has her maiden name. A rent receipt, a copy of her lease, and her voter registration were also rejected. Thelma Mitchell, a 93-year-old woman who worked for years cleaning the state capital, including the governor's office, was denied because she couldn't produce a birth certificate, having been birthed by a midwife in 1918. When she told that to a DMV clerk, she was suspected of being an illegal immigrant. Now that's rich. Some voting arbiter imagined this old woman trying to sneak into a voting booth, perhaps having just trundled through miles of desert to stake her claim in America. It's a good thing we have these gatekeepers at the ready, protecting the sanctity of our democratic system from infiltrating 93-year-olds.

Working to restrict voting is bad enough, but how about ignoring the electoral process entirely and allowing a governor to appoint city managers at his or her own discretion, whenever it's the opinion of that governor that the municipality isn't being run properly? Think it couldn't happen in America? Think again. That's exactly what Michigan Governor Rick Snyder tried to pull off with the vaguely titled Public Act 4, better known as the Emergency Manager Law. This insult to representative democracy gave the Republican governor the power to appoint managers to head cities he deemed fiscally irresponsible. A liberal group, Stand Up for Democracy, is doing just that (standing up for democracy, that is), fighting against what amounts to overturning legal elections. Under Snyder's law, his appointees were given the right to overturn union contracts and take power away from duly elected public officials. The governor would also be able to enter into contracts with no legislative oversight, seize and sell public assets without court orders, and dissolve or merge cities, townships, and school districts without a popular vote. When this was done in Benton Harbor, it turned out the real agenda was to build a golf course. Flint had better luck, as a judge kicked out Snyder's handpicked city manager. Ingham County Circuit Court Judge Rosemarie Aquilina restored the mayor and the city council—the very folks who had been democratically elected—once she realized secret meetings to overturn the will of the voters violated the Open Meeting Act. The Stand Up for Democracy coalition gathered hundreds of thousands of signatures to stop what they accurately describe as a "naked power grab."

What should be most telling is that laws that would result in fewer voters, such as those requiring voter ID, are almost always favored by Republicans and opposed by Democrats, such as what happened in Michigan, where the move to overturn elections was favored by a Republican governor and opposed by Democrats and liberal groups. Why is it that one side of the spectrum universally favors policies that would keep more people participating in the political process, while the other side almost universally, fights to disempower people? Doesn't this tell us who the true champions of our representative democracy are?

Remember, remember always, that all of us, and you and I especially, are descended from immigrants and revolutionists. ~*Franklin D. Roosevelt*

Another underappreciated group of people who contribute greatly to our well-being with little acknowledgment are immigrants, both legal and otherwise. For years, immigrants were accepted as part of our ever-expanding culture. How many of us can claim ancestors who arrived on the Mayflower? In fact, ask almost any anti-immigration conservative where his or her grandparents were born, and there's a good chance that person's stake in America is only a generation or two old. Immigration became more of a hot-button issue only when the immigrants were darker-skinned pilgrims from the south of us, not more culturally similar émigrés from the north. The influx of new Americans should be welcomed. This is part of America's identity and history. But some anti-immigrant activists would probably like to have a dome over the country as well, so we could be hermetically sealed and keep out the rest of the world. Pat Buchanan, for example, would like to stop all immigration, period—at least until unemployment is down to 6 percent.

Of course, the class of immigrants that is particularly controversial is "illegal immigrants," which has been shortened to the more pejorative "illegals" when used as a noun. Granted, this is a step up from "illegal alien," which makes it sound as though we're talking about someone from another planet. A growing number of liberals disdain the word *illegal* when applied to a person. To characterize a human being this way diminishes and condemns that person. I prefer *undocumented worker*, for that is what really defines the issue.

More than anyone, these needy souls personify Emma Lazarus's words at the base of the Statue of Liberty, "Give me your tired, your poor/Your huddled masses yearning to breathe free." Those words welcomed millions of huddled masses who arrived on our shores and built our nation, documented or not. They include my grandparents. And my father. And likely someone whose arrival here makes your life as good as it is today. These émigrés, like every other human being, deserve our respect.

It's fashionable to blame foreigners who didn't enter America through legal channels for all that ails us. If only these creepy, criminal laggards would stop invading our country, we could all have jobs and live happily ever after, the reasoning goes. Besides, the immigrant-bashers scream, wouldn't you toss out anyone who broke into your house? But unlike criminals who force entry to your home to steal from you, workers "break in" to America to get jobs and make better lives for themselves and their families. In the process, they give us better lives, too. They are highly motivated, with a strong work ethic, and make great sacrifices to be here, risking their lives, separating from their families, and living in squalid conditions that few Americans would or could endure. And contrary to what you may believe, they aren't eating up all our resources. They can't receive welfare, food stamps, or housing benefits. Medicare and Medicaid are not available to them. They can, however, receive education and emergency medical services.

Many of these "undocumented" persons are more American than we give them credit for. The Pew Hispanic Center released data at the end of 2011 showing that 60 percent of adult illegal immigrants have been in the country for a decade or more, and half of them have minor children. An additional 28 percent have been here from 10 to 14 years. Shall we pull them up by the roots they've developed and destroy their families?

There have been efforts, such as the Dream Act, to allow undocumented residents to get college educations. "Dream" is a wonderful way to put it; it stands for

Development, Relief, and Education for Alien Minors, and it would allow those who came here as minors, have lived here for at least five years, and have graduated from high school to become permanent residents. With two years in either the military or in a four-year institution of higher learning, there would be a pathway to citizenship. This bill was initially put forth in 2001 by liberal Illinois Senator Dick Durbin and conservative Utah Senator Orrin Hatch. Although discussion was postponed a number of times, Durbin and other Democrats continued to push for it, while the conservatives who initially supported the bill—such as Hatch and Senators John McCain, Lindsey Graham, Jon Kyl, and John Cornyn—turned against it on the pretext that it shouldn't be passed without stronger immigration enforcement, even though stronger enforcement was taking place concurrently. Florida Congressman Allen West went so far as to call a hearing Durbin conducted on this bill "reprehensible" and "treasonous" because of Durbin's view that those who are now seen as illegal immigrants could be our future leaders or even a future president.

But liberals supporting the Dream Act were right in line with the conservative belief in fiscal responsibility. The Congressional Budget Office and the Joint Committee on Taxation said that the November 2010 version of the bill would have increased government revenues by $2.3 billion over ten years and reduced the deficit by $1.4 billion by 2020.

Even Texas Governor Rick Perry, not exactly a liberal icon, signed a Texas version of this legislation, recognizing the need to make sure that immigrants on our soil have access to education. The California Dream Act was passed in 2011 and signed into law by Governor Jerry

Brown for this same reason. It's in our interest to see that everyone in America, no matter how he or she got here, is well educated and prepared to contribute to the work force (or, in Republican terms, the tax base).

Jason Riley, who sits on the editorial board of *The Wall Street Journal*, wrote *Let Them In: The Case For Open Borders* in 2008. As he told Stephen Colbert when he went on his show to promote his book, "If you want to reduce illegal immigration, give them more legal ways to come." The character Colbert plays, in all its wisdom, wanted to know if we could at least keep them separate, pleading, "Can we put individual walls around them?" If conservatives had their way, I bet they would do exactly that to immigrants already here.

Entering America without papers isn't quite law-breaking in the conventional sense. Fox News Senior Judicial Analyst Andrew Napolitano argues that coming to the country without papers disobeys an administrative rule, but it is not a crime. Besides, reasoned Judge Napolitano in an e-mail exchange with me, "A border is an artificial and imaginary line drawn as a political compromise by people who were prepared to kill each other over the location of the line and who are now dead. How can an imaginary line possibly interfere with one's humanity?"

Conservative arguments against immigration play on fear. They claim immigrants are here to take jobs from hard-working Americans and ruin our economy by taking advantage of our policies without giving anything back. But those arguments ignore the facts. These would-be countrymen aren't killing our economy—far from it. In fact, they contribute to it by doing work our citizens won't touch and they otherwise enhance our general well-being, as evidenced by demonstrable data. Don't take it from me, an immigrant-loving liberal; take it from the libertarian Cato Institute, which has done numerous studies on the impact of undocumented workers. Legalizing 8 million of them would economically benefit America, increasing the gross domestic product 1.27 percent, and adding $160 billion to the economy. A 2009 report by Maureen Rimmer and Peter Dixon states what deporting them would mean: "Modest savings in public expenditures would be more than offset by losses in economic output and job opportunities for more skilled American workers. A policy that reduces the number of low-skilled immigrant workers by 28.6 percent, compared to projected levels, would reduce U.S. household welfare by about 0.5 percent, or $80 billion." The Center for American Progress estimates that mass deportation would reduce the country's Gross Domestic Product by 1.46 percent, which would amount to $2.6 trillion in cumulative losses over ten years.

During the last few years, a number of states have passed very restrictive immigration laws, leading to the improper deportation of American citizens. An October 2011 study by the Warren Institute at UC Berkeley (named after former Supreme Court Justice Earl Warren) revealed that the Secure Communities Program started in 2008 by ICE (U.S. Immigration and Customs Enforcement) resulted in the arrest of 3,600 United States citizens, more than a third of whom had a child or spouse who is a citizen. This study also highlights the targets of many of the restrictive new laws: 93 percent of those arrested were Latinos, even though they represent just 77 percent of the undocumented population in the United States. Another study, by Jacqueline Stevens of

Northwestern University, revealed that 4,000 American citizens were deported in 2010, and more than 20,000 Americans have been deported since 2003. These are all wrongful arrests, as immigration authorities don't have the right to arrest American citizens. To correct this problem, ICE, under President Obama, instituted a hotline so citizens falsely arrested on immigration violations could have recourse. Its purpose is "to ensure that individuals being held by state or local law enforcement on immigration detainers are properly notified about their potential removal from the country and are made aware of their rights." While conservatives view this as giving "rights" to illegal immigrants, what it really does is protect American citizens who are too often falsely arrested and accused of being in the country illegally. Again, it's about protecting the innocent rather than punishing the guilty.

When it was passed in 2010, Arizona's immigration law, SB 1070, was one of the strictest in the nation. It required officials to determine the immigration status of anyone they stop for any reason, if there is any suspicion the detainee is here illegally. And that person can't be released until his or her immigration status is determined. This law also made it a state crime for illegal immigrants to fail to register with the federal government. Arizona wanted to make it a crime for these immigrants to work or even to try to find work. The federal government makes it illegal for employers to hire undocumented workers, but the workers themselves are subject only to civil—not criminal—penalties. Even more troubling, SB 1070 gives police the power to arrest anyone they suspect of doing anything worthy of deportation under federal law, with no warrant required. As Texas Congresswoman Sheila Jackson Lee put it, "So when a family gets into a car in Arizona—Tucson, Phoenix, and other beautiful places—and drives for a Sunday service, a mass, a picnic, you've now vested innocently in law enforcement officers, who all of us respect, the right to be judge and jury."

Once again, liberals stepped up to fight against this travesty of justice. The Department of Justice filed suit against Arizona's SB 1070 law saying that it "sets a state-level immigration policy that interferes with federal administration and enforcement of the immigration laws," thus violating the supremacy clause laid out in the Constitution. This clause states that federal laws are the supreme law of the land and laws made at the state level cannot overrule laws put in place by the federal government. Seven Democratic state attorneys general and close to 70 Democratic members of Congress filed amicus briefs in support of the federal government's lawsuit against Arizona's SB 1070. New York State Attorney General Eric Schneiderman pointed to Article I, Section 8 of the Constitution, which gives Congress the power "to establish a uniform rule of naturalization." Having uniform enforcement policies promotes fairness, which is why immigration enforcement is the job of the feds. But there are things a state can do for the benefit of all its citizens. Schneiderman spoke eloquently about the federal/state divide on the undocumented worker issue when he said, "The states have decisions to make about how you treat people, how your welfare system operates, your school system, your criminal justice system. How you treat people in your borders—that's the province of the state. The decision of who gets into the country and who is expelled from the country is very different."

SB 1070 was promoted with the argument that illegal immigrants increase crime. Cato's Daniel Griswold reports how those fears are misguided: "The crime rate in Arizona in 2008 was the lowest it has been in four decades. In the past decade, as the number of illegal immigrants in the state grew rapidly, the violent crime rate dropped by 23 percent, the property crime rate by 28 percent." Griswold also reports that immigrants in general are less likely to commit crime than their native-born counterparts. He studied the effect of cracking down on illegal immigration in the state of Pennsylvania and in September 2011 found that "removing low-skilled immigrant workers from the labor force would reduce investment and production in such industries as agriculture, retail, tourism, construction, and landscaping. It would reduce the related job openings in more skilled positions, reducing employment for native-born middle-class Americans. Less investment and employment would in turn reduce government revenue." Harsh anti-immigration laws in Alabama have caused farmers hardships, as undocumented workers fled the state, greatly reducing available labor to harvest crops.

Undocumented workers give far more to America than they ever get back. They can't receive food stamps, Medicare, or Medicaid; they don't eat up social services. In fact, they often try to have as little as possible to do with government for fear of getting caught. They do receive ITIN (Individual Tax Identification Number) cards from the IRS to pay taxes. And let's not forget that their presence in the workforce gives us lower prices for items like food, and cheaper construction costs. Far from hurting us, they contribute to our well-being, all too often more than we contribute to theirs.

The amount of money and of legal energy being given to prosecute hundreds of thousands of Americans who are caught with a few ounces of marijuana in their jeans simply makes no sense . . . It is an outrage, an imposition on basic civil liberties and on the reasonable expenditure of social energy. *~William F. Buckley, Jr.*

The Right and the Left have a great divide on how to deal with drugs and the people who are addicted to them. These are people who need help, not prison. Locking people up because they have addictions doesn't solve the drug problem. It crowds our prisons and costs us money. But in 1971, President Richard Nixon officially declared a "War on Drugs," identifying drug abuse as "public enemy No. 1." This led to the 1973 creation of the Drug Enforcement Administration. It wasn't until Jimmy Carter campaigned for President in 1976 that a more enlightened view was publicly expressed. Carter wanted to decriminalize marijuana and end federal penalties for possession of up to an ounce of the herb. But when our next Republican President, Ronald Reagan, took power, the drug war continued. Nancy Reagan's suggestion to "Just Say No" wasn't all that easy for young people influenced by peer pressure, or for those who were already addicts.

President Reagan spent $1.7 billion on the War on Drugs under the Anti-Drug Abuse Act of 1986. And mandatory minimum penalties became contentious because of the disparity between sentences for crack and for powder cocaine. Possession of less expensive crack resulted in harsher penalties for its users, who tended to be a racially diverse, lower-income group. When George H. W. Bush became President he created the Office of National Drug Control Policy and appointed Bill Bennett the nation's first "drug czar." Bennett and many other conservatives continue to argue that drugs must be kept illegal in order to keep them from falling into the hands of children, as well as to reduce violence and eliminate drug dealers. However, after decades of a failed drug war, it should be apparent that these policies haven't produced the intended results. The War on Drugs hasn't stopped young (or older) people from using them, nor has it reduced violence or eliminated the drug cartels. And we should have learned from our history with alcohol that prohibition doesn't work, which is why the Eighteenth Amendment to our Constitution was overturned by the Twenty-first Amendment. Thankfully, failures of the drug war have begun to give way to more enlightened views.

The first drug court was created in 1989 in Miami by then-State Attorney Janet Reno; users could be ordered into treatment rather than sent to jail. The Obama administration has greatly increased funding for drug courts, which have proven to reduce dependency. The Urban Institute reports that recidivism rates for those who graduate from drug court vary between 4 percent and 29 percent, as opposed to 48 percent for those who don't have this opportunity.

Not every conservative embraced the War on Drugs the way Nixon, Reagan, Bush 41, and Bennett did. The Second Chance Act, signed into law by President George W. Bush, provided money to communities for reentry services for former addicts, and the federal government urged local housing authorities to give consideration to former drug users returning from prison. Should we add W to the liberal column?

In addition to the funding of drug courts, the Obama administration instituted some of the most progressive drug policies we've ever had, recognizing that drug use is more a disease than a crime. As a result, $10.4 billion was spent on drug prevention and treatment in fiscal year 2011, versus $9.2 billion on domestic drug enforcement, according to the Office of National Drug Control Policy. I mentioned in Chapter 2 that President Obama signed the Fair Sentencing Act into law, reducing a 100 to 1 disparity between sentences for powder cocaine and those for crack cocaine to 18 to 1. Democrats were the driving force behind evening up the score, although a more progressive bill pushed by Republican Ron Paul and Democrat Dennis Kucinich would have made the penalties for powder and crack cocaine equal.

Former New Mexico Republican Governor Gary Johnson looks at the issue of drug use from a cost-benefit point of view. "We have the highest incarceration rate of any country in the world, that's on a per capita basis," Johnson told a crowd during his 2012 run for the White House. "Half of what we spend on law enforcement, the courts, and the prisons is drug related. We're arresting 1.8 million people a year in this country on drug-related crime." Johnson's views are clearly much less authoritarian than the Republican platform. Because of how the Republican Party shunned him during the 2012 presidential race, he left the GOP and won the Libertarian Party nomination for president.

The Office of National Drug Control Policy reports that between 1988 and 2009, corrections spending on the state level increased from $12 billion to more than $50 billion per year. A study by the RAND Corporation in the '90s found that every dollar spent on drug treatment saved $7.50 in reduced crime and productivity.

Harvard economist Jeffrey Miron, also a libertarian, has done much work analyzing the economic and social costs of drug prohibition, which, he opines, make no sense economically. In a 2010 white paper for the CATO Institute Miron offered a cost/benefit analysis of drug legalization:

> This report estimates that legalizing drugs would save roughly $41.3 billion per year in government expenditure on enforcement of prohibition. Of these savings, $25.7 billion would accrue to state and local governments, while $15.6 billion would accrue to the federal government.
>
> Approximately $8.7 billion of the savings would result from legalization of marijuana and $32.6 billion from legalization of other drugs.
>
> The report also estimates that drug legalization would yield tax revenue of $46.7 billion annually, assuming legal drugs were taxed at rates comparable to those on alcohol and tobacco. Approximately $8.7 billion of this revenue would result from legalization of marijuana and $38.0 billion from legalization of other drugs.

Miron also did a 2003 study on the economic costs of drug abuse that pointed out the consequences of our current policy of prohibition and incarceration:

- increased violence and corruption
- diminished civil liberties
- heightened racial tensions
- distorted foreign relations

- added restrictions on medical drug use
- the transfer of wealth to criminals
- civil unrest within drug-producing countries

Besides, wrote Miron in 2009, "prohibition has disastrous implications for national security. By eradicating coca plants in Colombia or poppy fields in Afghanistan, prohibition breeds resentment of the United States. By enriching those who produce and supply drugs, prohibition supports terrorists who sell protection services to drug traffickers."

The Center for Economic and Policy research found in 2010 that nonviolent offenders made up more than 60 percent of the country's prison population and accounted for about one-fourth of all offenders behind bars, up from less than 10 percent in 1980. Our Department of Justice has data that shows that two-thirds of drug offenders who are released from prison will be arrested again within three years, just continuing the cycle. Never mind what side of the plate you're on politically, doesn't it make the most sense to have a policy that best helps people, reduces the problem, and costs the least? We're starting to move in this direction, thanks to the liberals.

When I was in the military they gave me a medal for killing two men and a discharge for loving one.
~*Leonard P. Matlovich*

Great controversy has always surrounded what public policies should be toward the poor, undocumented immigrants, and drug users. These groups are often lumped together as an underclass with little political or economic clout. One other group that has historically fit this description—although it is emerging as a more powerful social and economic force—is the LGBT (lesbian, gay, bisexual, transgender) community. As they gain more economic clout, they are slowly gaining long-fought-for and much-deserved equal rights, particularly in the area of marriage equality.

"Have You Thanked a Liberal Today?" took us through the legislative and court battles for privacy, gender equality, and sexual freedom that have finally resulted in gays serving in the military and some states permitting gay marriage. But if America has issues (and it does—don't we all?), this is a fast-changing one; even President Obama, who has traditionally favored domestic partnerships over gay marriage, said his views were "evolving," and they did so quickly, as he announced his support for marriage equality in May 2012.

Sadly, too many of our public officials, including would-be presidents, are devolving. Let's look at what's been said during the 2012 presidential campaign.

Rick Santorum got the most support of any 2012 candidate from evangelicals and social conservatives, and his views on gay marriage were no small part of that. He called traditional marriage the "ultimate homeland security," as though straight marriage would protect us from another 9/11. In 2005, *The New York Times Magazine* writer Michael Sokolove asked Santorum if he viewed gay marriage as a threat to his own marriage. The answer: "It threatens my marriage. It threatens all marriages. It threatens the traditional values of this country." I'm still trying to figure out how two same-sex people enjoying wedded bliss somehow gets in the way of my own relationship. Can someone explain this to me?

Santorum continued spending much time and political capital talking about gays after he left the Senate and as he moved into his run for president. In 2008, he compared gay marriage to incest, telling interviewer Michelangelo Signorile, "if it's all about equality" it would be okay for "a niece and an aunt . . . or a brother and a sister . . . Why not allow that to happen?" During one campaign stop, he said, "Unless we protect [the family] with the institution of marriage, our country will fall." When Pew Research came out with a survey showing fewer people were getting hitched, he tweeted, "Here is 1 effect of changing definition of marriage . . . Marriage rate in America drops to new low . . ." It's hard to fathom that allowing gays to marry would result in falling heterosexual marriage rates. I'm guessing gay people aren't running to city hall with members of the opposite sex when they're denied the right to marry the ones they love. Rick Santorum vowed that if elected president he'd support a Constitutional amendment to define marriage as between a man and a woman. When asked what this would mean for same-sex couples who have already been legally wed, he replied, "Well, their marriage would be invalid. . . If the constitution says 'Marriage is this,' then people whose marriages are not consistent with the constitution . . . (shrug.)" The problem with adding a restrictive definition of marriage to the Constitution is that it is utterly *un*-Constitutional. Rick Santorum, meet Amendment Fourteen, Section 1: "No State shall make or enforce any law which shall abridge the privileges or immunities of citizens of the United States; nor shall any State deprive any person of life, liberty, or property, without due process of law; nor deny to any person within its jurisdiction the equal protection of the laws." While campaigning in Iowa, Santorum was confronted by 23-year-old Jason Kornelis wanting to know how same-sex marriage could, quoting Santorum, "be a hit to faith and family in America." Santorum replied that if gay marriage were legal, gay sex would be seen as equal to straight sex: "If we say legally, if this type of relationship is identical to other type relationships, then of course more of it will be taught, because this is what the law says." In other words, if we say it's okay to be gay, the next thing you know, your schools are offering a course called Gay 101, probably with mandatory gay homework. Santorum also claimed if we allow gays to be parents, we're denying children the opportunity to have a mother and a father. This presumes there are a mother and a father to adopt every child who needs a home. It also presumes that the well-being of a family is based on the parents' gender. Can anyone honestly argue that a home with two heterosexual parents constantly at each others' throats is a better place for a child to be than in a home with same-gender parents who live in peace?

Michele Bachmann, she of the clinic that offers "gay reparative therapy," had an even tougher challenger on the campaign trail than did Rick Santorum—an 8-year-old named Elijah who didn't like her message. Bachmann fell silent when Elijah told her, "My mommy, Miss Bachmann, my mommy's gay, but she doesn't need fixing."

Mitt Romney spent the primary season searching for his inner conservative. Never mind that in 1994, when he was trying to unseat Senator Ted Kennedy, in a letter to the Log Cabin Republicans of Massachusetts, he vowed to be more progressive on gay rights than his opponent. Romney promised, "I am more convinced than ever before that as we seek to establish full equality for America's gay and lesbian citizens, I will provide more effective leadership than my opponent." But a funny thing happened on the way to the 2012 Republican nomination. When California's Proposition 8, which defined marriage as between a man and a woman, was declared unconstitutional, Romney blasted the decision and the judge, declaring, "I believe marriage is between a man and a woman and, as president, I will protect traditional marriage and appoint judges who interpret the Constitution as it is written and not according to their own politics and prejudices." Romney was taking a shot at U.S. District Judge Vaughn Walker, who happens to be gay, implying the judge was acting in self-interest when he ruled against Proposition 8. So who knows what Romney really thinks? It seems the only thing he believes in for sure is that he wants to be president.

I've noted throughout this book that in unguarded moments, or when the chips are no longer on the table, a politician or a political operative will reveal what he or she really thinks, and often that revelation shows how liberal that person really is. Ken Mehlman, who was George W. Bush's campaign manager, came out only after the Bush presidency was over, and only a couple of years after that did he express regret for his work in putting anti-gay initiatives on ballots in 2004: "At a personal level, I wish I had spoken out against the effort. As I've been involved in the fight for marriage equality, one of the things I've learned is how many people were harmed by the campaigns in which I was involved. I apologize to them and tell them I am sorry." No one would have expected George W. Bush's campaign manager to announce he's gay in the middle of a presidential run, but how amazing it would have been had Mehlman done this when he later headed the Republican National Committee. It's good that he came clean, stood up, and apologized, but he did so when there was little risk.

Ken Mehlman finally came to understand what more Americans are learning: why it's not okay to call a union between same-sex people anything other than "marriage." I get calls on my radio show all the time from people who have a real problem with calling same-sex unions "marriage." "Okay, we'll change the name," I'll say, replacing "m" with a "g" for "gay." "We'll call it 'garriage.'" That doesn't go over too well, either. Even one letter away feels too close for comfort to some people. Let's not forget that marriage wasn't created by God, but rather by man, to help deal with property rights. Adam and Eve didn't do contracts. And how could they have been married? No one else was around to perform the ceremony.

But even so, fights have been raging around this topic. When the Supreme Court of Hawaii, in the case of *Baehr v. Miike,* ruled that the state's refusal to grant marriage licenses to same-sex couples was discriminatory, conservatives started a full-fledged fight to combat the fear that Hawaii's more liberal views would infect the rest of the country. Republicans Bob Barr of Georgia in the House and Don Nickles of Oklahoma in the Senate introduced the Defense of Marriage Act (DOMA) to amend the U.S. Constitution to make sure marriage would be defined, once and for all, as between a man and a woman. Republicans rushed to put this in their 1996 platform to make sure the party faithful would *stay* faithful. This led Ted Kennedy to refer to DOMA as the

"Endangered Republican Candidates Act" and call it "a mean-spirited form of legislative gay-bashing." It had the support of many Democrats in both houses and was quickly signed by President Clinton, proving once again that "Democrat" doesn't always mean "liberal." This is yet another reminder to me as to why I'm a liberal who happens to be a Democrat rather than the other way around.

The Defense of Marriage Act didn't go far enough for some conservatives. President George W. Bush felt this way and wanted a constitutional amendment to make sure marriage would be forever limited to opposite sex couples. But when Barack Obama ran for president in 2008, his platform endorsed repeal of DOMA, and in 2011 Attorney General Eric Holder said that while the government would uphold the law, it would no longer defend it in court.

Marriage between same-sex partners was first made legal in the United States in 2003 in Massachusetts, when the state's Supreme Judicial Court ruled that the state could not "deny the protections, benefits, and obligations conferred by civil marriage to two individuals of the same sex who wish to marry." After it became legal for gays to marry in the Bay State, more than 6,000 couples married that same year. Then a combination of rulings by left-leaning state courts and laws promoted by liberal legislators made same-sex marriage more widespread. Gay marriage has been legal in Connecticut since November 2008, in Iowa since April 2009, and in Vermont since November 2009. New Hampshire made it legal as of January 2010, and New York came on board in July 2011. California has been a battleground on this issue since the state Supreme Court permitted same-sex marriage licenses in May 2008 in keeping with the Equal Protection Clause. Proposition 8 (known by its supporters as the Marriage Protection Act) was then passed in November 2008. This piece of loveliness would add wording to the California Constitution that "only marriage between a man and a woman is valid or recognized in California." However, an intense court battle ensued, keeping marriage equality in abeyance. Here you had 18,000 same-sex couples who were legally married in California before Prop 8 made such unions illegal. Between November 2008, when Prop 8 passed, and May 26, 2009, when the California Supreme Court upheld the validity of those marriages, these couples didn't know for sure if their unions were legal.

Marriage isn't just a word that's interchangeable with terms like *domestic partnership* or *civil union*. We can't call it something else and make believe it's the same thing. For one thing, domestic partners can't legally have children and be a family the same way a married couple can. Without marriage, couples are denied property ownership rights, joint bank accounts, child adoption, and the use of surrogate mothers. Should one partner die, rights of survivorship don't apply to couples unless they're married. The federal Government Accountability Office reports that there are 1,138 federal rights, protections, and responsibilities available only to those who are joined in matrimony. Add to the ones I just mentioned:

- Social Security benefits upon death, disability, or retirement of spouse, as well as benefits for minor children

- Family and Medical Leave protections to care for a new child or a sick or injured family member

- Workers' Compensation protections for the family of a worker injured on the job

- Access to COBRA insurance benefits so that the family doesn't lose health insurance when one spouse is laid off

- ERISA (Employee Retirement Income Security Act) protections, such as the ability to leave a pension other than Social Security to your spouse

- Exemptions from penalties on IRA and pension rollovers

- Exemptions from estate taxes when a spouse dies

- Exemptions from federal income taxes on spouse's health insurance

- The right to visit a sick or injured loved one and have a say in life-and-death matters during hospitalization

Until every state has the same marriage laws, gays can cross a state line and suddenly have their unions cast asunder by virtue of geography. But this is changing. And for the better.

There's so much pollution in the air now that if it weren't for our lungs there'd be no place to put it all.
~Robert Orben

Liberals fight for equal protection not just for all racial and sexual groups but for America itself. And by "America itself" I mean the very land we love and the very air we breathe. Liberals have spearheaded the fight for conservation and believe that as we are stewards of the earth, it is our responsibility to protect it. We are intertwined with our environment and each other, and only by realizing this can we live fruitfully and move toward a sustainable future.

Unfortunately, politics doesn't necessarily allow for a joint effort on saving the planet. Efforts to work together for the common good are poisoned by partisan politics and big money. And big money comes via big oil interests to think tanks that produce results that favor big oil. Energy expert Robert Rapier, author of *Power Plays: Energy Options in the Age of Peak Oil,* told my radio audience that the "drill here, drill now, drill, drill, drill" crowd needs to be reminded that if we drilled for the 18 billion barrels in the outer continental shelf of the lower 48 states, we'd have two and a half years worth of oil. Is that what's going to save us?

Jon Huntsman was the only 2012 Republican presidential candidate who came out in favor of something called "science." He tweeted, "To be clear, I believe in evolution and trust scientists on global warming. Call me crazy." Sadly, too many on the Right thought he was, and he was relegated to the back of the candidate pack. Rick Santorum argued, "Science should get out of politics." No, Rick, it's the other way around. When Newt Gingrich was a candidate, he accused President Obama of wanting high gas prices on purpose. That was all going to a change with a Gingrich presidency, which, the former Speaker vowed, would deliver $2.50-a-gallon gas. Nice try, but he knows that's not how the market works. Besides, Michele Bachmann had already promised $2-a-gallon gas and look what happened to her campaign. Speculation, instability in the Middle East, and a global market we don't control determine gas prices, not an Oval-Office price dictator. But heaven forbid facts should get in the way of a political agenda. Truth is a harsh mistress, so let's get some facts on the table.

On January 27, 2012, *The Wall Street Journal* ran an op-ed by 16 scientists claiming global warming was not an important issue, hadn't existed for a decade, and was "smaller than predicted." Nearly two years earlier, 255 scientists, all members of the National Academy of Sciences, published a letter in *Science* magazine with information originally offered to the *Journal*, which had turned it down. They shared findings that directly contradicted the claims in the 2012 *Journal* article:

- The planet is warming due to increased concentrations of heat-trapping gases in our atmosphere. A snowy winter in Washington does not alter this fact.

- Most of the increase in the concentration of these gases over the last century is due to human activities, especially the burning of fossil fuels and deforestation.

- Natural causes always play a role in changing Earth's climate but are now being overwhelmed by human-induced changes.

- Warming the planet will cause many other climatic patterns to change at speeds unprecedented in modern times, including increasing rates of sea-level rise and alterations in the hydrologic cycle. Rising concentrations of carbon dioxide are making the oceans more acidic.

- The combination of these complex climate changes threatens coastal communities and cities, our food and water supplies, marine and freshwater ecosystems, forests, high mountain environments, and far more.

Professor Bill McKibben of Middlebury College and grist.com debunked the *Journal* article. Five of the scientists, he discovered, had ties to Exxon, for one thing. Oil companies like ExxonMobil are valued on the basis of fossil-fuel reserves that will never be burned if global warming is taken seriously. With a 2011 profit of $41 billion, ExxonMobil isn't going softly into that good night. And, as McKibben notes, money wins over chemistry and physics. And much oil industry money goes into Republican coffers. Opensecrets.org reports that even as other traditionally right-leaning industries begin to open up their wallets for the Left, "this sector has remained rock-solid red."

Al Gore has been at the forefront of educating us about climate change. And the United Nations Intergovernmental Panel on Climate Change regularly assesses information put out by the scientific community, showing the effects of human-induced climate change. This rankles conservatives if only because of their general antipathy for Gore, and for the United Nations and all it represents. Unfortunately for the deniers, it's not about the U.N. or any one person or group; it's about science.

The National Oceanic and Atmospheric Administration's *2010 State of the Climate* report is consistent with studies from other recent years, stating, among other things:

1. Three data sets show global surface temperatures continue to rise; 2010 was one of the two warmest years on record.

2. Air samples collected weekly at NOAA's Mauna Loa observatory continue to show a rise in the concentration of carbon dioxide.

3. Greenland's ice sheet lost more mass in 2010 than at any time in the past ten years.

4. Trends in snow-cover duration, permafrost, and vegetation continued or accelerated.

In addition, sea levels continued to rise in the world's oceans; ocean heat content was similar to that of 2009 (2009 and 2010 are two of the highest years on record); average surface temperature on the world's oceans was the third warmest on record; the world's mountain glaciers lost mass for the 20th consecutive year; and Arctic sea ice shrank to its third smallest area on record.

In 2011, NOAA reported that it was the 35th straight year that the yearly global temperature was above the 20th-century average. The Global Carbon Project, an international consortium of scientists, reports that in 2010, global emissions of carbon dioxide jumped by the largest amount on record, rising 5.9 percent. And we have a carbon bubble, having used a third of our 50-year carbon budget in 2011, according to carbontracker.org. Climate genius Mitt Romney explained this during his campaign: "I exhale carbon dioxide." This explains increased levels of CO_2: so many people sighing about the chance he might one day be President caused the level of exhalations to reach unprecedented levels.

Conservatives thought they had a "gotcha" moment in 2009 when e-mails exchanged between scientists at the Climatic Research Unit at the UK's University of East Anglia contained some phrases that, when taken out of context, made it seem as though the experts there were trying to cover up evidence that global warming isn't real. One sentence was all they needed to go on the attack. Phil Jones, head of the unit, wrote, "I have just completed Mike's Nature trick of adding in the real temps to each series for the last 20 years . . . to hide the decline." Climate change deniers went "Aha! See? They are using tricks to hide that temperatures are declining." But that was not what that sentence meant. Jones was referring to Penn State climatologist Michael Mann's studies on temperature that show a warming trend from 1900 to the time of the e-mail, 1999. Between 1000 and 1960, studies of tree rings were used to determine temperatures, but after 1960, thermometer readings were used, and that's when it shows things really began to heat up. Mann says the word "trick" was not deception, but rather a "trick of the trade" scientists use to get reliable data. Because of pollution and other factors, tree-ring data was less reliable after 1960, and so a different method was used. The "decline" refers to a decline in temperatures in the unreliable tree-ring data. But why should context matter when you have a political agenda driven by big-money interests? Let the record be set straight.

If liberals are to save America, there must first be a planet that's saved. While the Right and its moneyed interests choose denial, an administration that is progressive on the environment and grassroots groups that believe in science over emotionalism are taking action. Thanks to the Obama administration, if you put solar panels on your house or a turbine wind system on your property, you can get tax credits for 30 percent of the cost through 2016. In March 2012, the administration announced stringent rules to limit power plant carbon dioxide emissions. These power plants account for 40 percent of the nation's CO_2 output. The new rules—that emissions must be in line with natural gas technology—virtually guarantee that old coal plants are a thing of the past. In July 2011, the Obama administration announced new car and light-truck fuel-efficiency standards that will begin to apply in 2017 and, by 2025, will require performance equal to 54.5 miles per gallon. Greenhouse gas emissions will be reduced by 163 grams per mile. A month later, new standards were announced for commercial vehicles. These rules will reduce oil usage by 530 million barrels between 2014 and 2018 and save a trucker $73,000 in fuel costs during the life of a truck.

Community groups like RiverKeeper in New York have advocated for cleaner water and protecting the ecology of the Hudson River. After years of advocacy by RiverKeeper and a 70-group collective called SWIM Coalition, New York City agreed to invest $3.8 billion over 18 years to prevent sewage from flowing into the area's waterways. Even in the small town of Freeman, South Dakota, there is a movement called Rural Revival that is educating citizens about conservation and promoting organic farming and farmers' markets. This not only motivates citizens to have a sense of community and good environmental practices but also helps support local farmers. The Iowa-based Farmers' Market Coalition does similar work by bringing together farmers and consumers so that by finding each other, the farmers develop a market for their goods, and consumers get fresh, nutritious local produce while supporting their communities. It's interesting to note that these grassroots groups don't present themselves as liberals but are acting in ways that simply make sense for preserving their land and their communities. This is another wonderful example of how, when you take ideology and money out of the equation, people act in ways divorced from identity politics.

You cannot simultaneously prevent and prepare for war. ~Albert Einstein

To the need to protect our most vulnerable citizens and our precious environment let's add the protection of our homeland. We've come through a decade of war, having lost more Americans in response to 9/11 than were killed on that actual date. The Afghanistan conflict is the longest war in our history, having surpassed the length of the Vietnam War in spring 2010. Vietnam lasted 8 years, 5 months. Besides adding to the bankrupting of America, our presence in other sovereign nations, often uninvited, doesn't exactly endear us to the rest of the world. Globally, we have 611 military instillations with many military members deployed based on the geopolitics of World War II. *Washington Post* fact checker Glenn Kessler notes that as of September 2011, we had 53,766 military personnel in Germany, 39,222 in Japan, 10,801 in Italy, and 9,382 in the United Kingdom. If we reapportioned our military population based on current-day needs, think of the money we could save.

This goes as well for choosing our wars more carefully. You'd think the lessons of the last ten years would have taught us the value of caution before committing America's youth and dollars to what became exercises in futility. Those who argue we're a "Christian nation" ought to consider the Just War theory as put forth by

St. Augustine, Cicero, and Thomas Aquinas. Wars, it was reasoned, should have philosophical, ethical, and even religious underpinnings for them to be justified. Six factors figure into the Just War theory:

1. There has to be a just cause, such as to defend oneself or stop aggression.

2. Right Intention is necessary so that war is not for a power grab or to advance selfish interests.

3. Proper authority must be used in the declaration of war, such as obeying a country's Constitution.

4. War must be a last resort; all other means of settlement have to be exhausted.

5. War can't be an act of futility; there must be a probability of success.

6. There must be proportionality. Potential casualties must be assessed on a universal scale. Losses and depletion of not just one's own resources but also those of the opposition and third parties must be considered.

Not only would we save treasure in both lives and money, but also we'd burnish our international reputation were we to use these guidelines before putting Americans in harm's way in the name of trying to shock and awe the rest of the world.

Part of the Bush Doctrine was that the United States could go wherever it deemed a nation might be a threat. The National Security Strategy issued on September 17, 2002, by the Bush administration set the stage for the Iraq invasion and, for the first time ever, codified the policy of preemptive war. It stated: "To forestall or prevent . . . hostile acts by our adversaries, the United States will, if necessary, act preemptively in exercising our inherent right of self-defense." I would argue that what the Bush administration was really doing was expressing a policy of preventive war, as the foreword to the 2002 NSS defines it: "As a matter of common sense and self-defense, America will act against such emerging threats before they are fully formed." While preemptive war means acting when there is believed to be an immediate threat, preventive war carries no such caveat and is a violation of international law. But George W. Bush's legal advisors, notably John Yoo and Robert Delahunty, had no problem telling the administration that this was acceptable.

Under President Obama, our National Security Strategy became much more in line with America's need to promote peace and sustainability. The May 2010 version called for more global engagement and eliminated phrases like "the global war on terror" and "Islamic extremism." Other foreign policy initiatives ruffled the Right but were in our long-term best interests. Obama came under fire from conservatives when he said that he was willing to talk to Iran "without preconditions" and that there would be a willingness to "talk to our foes and friends." During the 2008 campaign, President Obama and Vice President Joe Biden reasoned that "if America is willing to come to the table, the world will be more willing to rally behind American leadership to deal with challenges like confronting terrorism, and Iran and North Korea's nuclear programs." It was a radical departure from previous administrations, particularly the one right before it, when the Obama–Biden team brought a much more enlightened view to foreign policy.

Sadly, bluster emanating from those with political agendas during the 2012 presidential campaign was more in line with preventive war than with the more beatific teachings of St. Augustine. Listening to the candidates, you'd think we'd better head for the nearest fallout shelter. Newt Gingrich warned, "I would also point out that a Gingrich presidency would communicate publicly to the Iranians that if they continue to do what they're doing, they should expect to get hit, and it will be their fault for having caused it." Rick Santorum hyped to the American Israel Public Affairs Committee (AIPAC), "If Iran doesn't get rid of nuclear facilities, we will tear them down ourselves." Mitt Romney told the same group, "I will make sure Iran knows of the very real peril that awaits if it becomes nuclear." Another speech had Romney declaring, "If Barack Obama gets reelected, Iran will have a nuclear weapon, and the world will change if that's the case." In a *Washington Post* op-ed he vowed, "Either the ayatollahs will get the message, or they will learn some very painful lessons about the meaning of American resolve." What would we do if potential leaders of another country made these comments about us? I'm guessing we'd throw billions of dollars at the nearest defense contractor and start building weapons. Aren't we encouraging Iran to do the same? In Romney's editorial he also vowed, "I will take every measure necessary to check the evil regime of the ayatollahs. Until Iran ceases its nuclear-bomb program, I will press for ever-tightening sanctions, acting with other countries if we can but alone if we must. I will speak out on behalf of the cause of democracy in Iran and support

Iranian dissidents who are fighting for their freedom. I will make clear that America's commitment to Israel's security and survival is absolute." That all sounds so sane and rational, which it is. And that's probably why President Obama was already doing it.

Ron Paul was the only Republican nominee during the 2012 presidential campaign who was speaking out against unnecessary wars. As Paul has said, "Another term for preventive war is aggressive war—starting wars because someday, somebody might do something to us. That is not part of the American tradition." In the desire to trump up an excuse to invade Iraq, the House International Relations Committee drafted Joint Resolution 75, which stated that if Iraq refused to allow UN inspectors to act freely, it would be regarded as an "act of aggression against the United States." That language, tantamount to a war declaration, was removed before the final version, which stated Iraq represented a "mounting threat." Ron Paul wisely took to the House floor to say, "I strongly oppose House Joint Resolution 75 because it solves none of our problems and only creates new ones . . . Absent Iraqi involvement in the attack on the United States, I can only wonder why so many in Congress seek to divert resources away from our efforts to bring those who did attack us to justice. That hardly seems a prudent move."

It wasn't only the candidates (with the exception of Ron Paul) who beat the drums of war. Senate Minority Leader Mitch McConnell told APIAC, "If, at any time, the intelligence community presents the Congress with an assessment that Iran has begun to enrich uranium to weapons-grade levels, or has taken a decision to develop a nuclear weapon—consistent with protecting classified sources and methods—I will consult with the President and joint congressional leadership and introduce before the Senate an authorization for the use of military force." The last time there was such an authorization, it led to the Iraq war. And without invoking the War Powers Clause of that old document we like to call the Constitution.

Inflammatory rhetoric by those looking to score political points isn't what's going to change the world for the better. North Korea is now saying it wants a better relationship with the United States because it is no longer ruled by the unstable Kim Jong-il. In March 2012, the new regime agreed to suspend uranium enrichment and enacted a moratorium on nuclear and long-range missile tests. Secretary of State Hillary Clinton was correct to be hopeful yet to express "profound concerns." Donald Gregg, George H. W. Bush's ambassador to South Korea, acknowledged this development as "significant." But the far right wing couldn't accept this as a step forward. Former U.N. Ambassador John Bolton called it "a sham," and the Hudson Institute's Jack David said it was "worse than bad." Some people won't take "yes" for an answer, especially if credit for the "yes" goes to a political adversary.

It's notable that Kim's death and the transition of power in Pyongyang weren't the result of an American incursion. Similarly, the Arab Spring, beginning with the Egyptian uprising, occurred organically without United States interference. Wherever we've tried to force change to promote our own brand of democracy, the results have been disastrous. Peace doesn't arrive at the point of a bayonet.

Operative for the longest time was Thomas Friedman's "Golden Arches Theory of Conflict Prevention." In his 1999 book *The Lexus and the Olive Tree*, Friedman posited that no two countries that have McDonald's franchises go to war against each other. The middle class that allows McDonald's to bloom, he reasons, would rather be eating hamburgers than fighting wars. The 2008 South Ossetia War between Russia and Georgia proved that battles between countries with those golden arches are possible, but Friedman's greater point remains. But an even more potent force has arisen since *The New York Times* columnist presented his theory. With Twitter and Facebook connecting the world, a new generation of youths has eyes on the West, learning that another kind of life is possible and desirable. This, more than any army, will thwart dictatorships and end wars. More can be accomplished in 140 characters than in 140 days of war.

That doesn't mean that the making of democracies is pretty. Great meals come from messy kitchens. As the Arab Spring bloomed in Egypt, conservatives in America warned of the rise of the Muslim Brotherhood and how it would take over Egypt and other countries experiencing political upheaval. Although the Brotherhood is a movement, not a political party, its adherents are building political organizations in the Middle East, many of which advocate for democratic reforms. Before we get too crazed about who might succeed dying Arab regimes, let us not forget that the formation of our own republic was not a neat and clean process. In fact, it still isn't. The American Revolutionary War that got us our independence resulted in 8,000 battle deaths and an estimated 17,000 more from starvation and disease. Why should we believe that other forming democracies would be created without danger? But it should not be our business to decide for them what forces should be victorious. We claim to favor democracy, but when a group we don't like wins as a result of the democratic process, we're quick to protest. Hamas won a majority of seats in the Palestinian Parliament in 2006, but we still classify them as a terrorist group. It's notable that Switzerland, the world's great peacekeeper, does not. We can't have it both ways, though—claiming to be champions of democracy but questioning its value when we don't get the results we want.

However, the world is changing faster than I can write this book. New alliances are being formed, and old ones are shifting; elections are taking place; generations are growing up, and new ones are being born. The global power of the Internet is creating organic change that we can never replicate using tools as old-fashioned as military weapons. Let's hope that in years to come, nuclear weapons will be considered as archaic as spears are now. Digitalization is the new atomic bomb. Because of its impact and its reach, a new world is being created before our very eyes that is making the state of many of the issues being discussed here quickly obsolete.

A LITTLE HELP TO FIGHT THE RIGHT

The Citizens United decision drastically changed what constitutes a person. Corporations are not people, my friend. Corporations and humans have different basic needs. Corporations need profits to survive. Humans need fresh air, fresh water, life, liberty, and the opportunity to pursue happiness.

President Obama's stimulus package helped poverty-stricken Americans have food to eat and to stay in their homes. Democrats battled Republicans to keep unemployment benefits for those who couldn't find work because of the recession. And because of these efforts, unemployment benefits hit a four-year low in April 2012.

Voter ID laws being pushed by Republicans address a problem that doesn't exist. Incidents of voter fraud are few. Their real agenda is to prevent registration of those likely to vote Democratic.

Immigrants, both legal and otherwise, are not a drain on the economy. They contribute to it.

Arizona's strict immigration law was based on the belief that illegal immigrants increase crime. In fact, the crime rate in Arizona was the lowest in four decades between 1998 and 2008.

The drug war has been a failure; it hasn't reduced drug use or related violence and hasn't ended the drug cartels.

We save money when we treat drug use as an illness rather than a crime. The Obama administration is spending more on prevention and treatment. Every dollar spent on treatment saves seven-and-a-half dollars in reduced crime and productivity.

Domestic partnerships don't cut it in terms of equality. There are more than 1,000 items in our legal code that pertain only to those who are married.

If we drilled everywhere possible for oil in the outer continental shelf of the lower 48 states, the supply would be just two and a half years' worth.

Multiple data sets show global temperatures continue to rise, as do sea levels and sea surface temperatures.

Oil companies are valued based on fossil fuel reserves that won't be used if global warming is taken seriously, thus those with ties to big oil tend to promote denial.

We've lost more Americans in wars in response to 9/11 than we lost on that day.

Digitalization enables us to address our issues faster and more efficiently, making a better, more liberal world.

CHAPTER SEVEN

YOU'RE WELCOME!

I don't mean to be arrogant here. Okay, maybe a little snarky, but all for a good cause. Why do I say we should thank the liberals for saving America? Because they already have. Because they've been doing it for almost 250 years, and because they are likely to keep doing so. The left–right conflicts we are having right now in our country are a continuation of the ones we've had for centuries. Over time, liberals have won those battles, and with that predictor, we will continue to do so. And these victories have benefited all of us. But the Right does keep striking back as it attempts to overturn or chip away at progress. The battles about abortion, gun rights, gay rights, race relations, global warming, the infusion of religion in politics, and—God (or your favorite deity) help us—birth control, rage on.

But let me change the word *they* in the above paragraph to *we*. While I have been making the distinction between left and right, I do believe that *we* can all take credit for the beautiful nation that America is today. After all, as I argued in Chapter 1, we are all liberal in America by virtue of birth or citizenship, and because by being here and living our American ideals, we are honoring our country's liberal history, traditions, and founders. We all claim belief in the vision of our forefathers and the values they laid out for us in our Constitution and Declaration of Independence. We are all living their liberal dream, even if not all of us see it that way. We are liberally enjoying our liberal faiths, or happily enjoying a progressive society where no faith at all is equally acceptable.

We Made Too Many Wrong Mistakes. ~*Yogi Berra*

Americans are awakening to a new day as we realize that some of what we once believed has turned out not to be true. We often mock the Flat Earth Society, but that is only one example of now-discredited beliefs. We humans also no longer believe that the Sun revolves around Earth, that our planet is just a couple of thousand years old, or that the universe can only expand so far. Until Isaac Newton's *Principia* in 1687, we didn't have a theory of gravity. Fast-forward to the present day, and we are hit almost daily with shocking reality checks that change our understanding of things and so give us new ways of looking at the world. As I've stated in these pages, liberals believe that with new information comes the need to change our thinking, and liberals more often than conservatives have shown the willingness to do so. That's not being wishy-washy, a word too often applied to liberals; it's being open-minded.

One recent case in point is the admission from Rafid Ahmed Alwan al-Janabi, the Iraqi chemical engineer whose claims we believed about his homeland having weapons of mass destruction. In April 2012, he finally revealed that his story was invented out of whole cloth. His calculated lies dragged the United States into a war based on his own agenda. He told BBC2's "Modern Spies" program: "My main purpose was to topple the tyrant in Iraq, because the longer this dictator remains in power, the more the Iraqi people will suffer from this regime's oppression." Then–Secretary of State Colin Powell risked his own legacy when he stood up at the United Nations and presented al-Janabi's information as "facts and conclusions based on solid intelligence." Just a few weeks earlier, President Bush, in his 2003 State of the Union address, told the nation about "several mobile biological weapons labs" that were also part of the defector's tissue of lies. When confronted by the BBC with the statement, "We went to war in Iraq on a lie. And that lie was your lie," al-Janabi's only response was "Yes." Next time, maybe we should take a clue and not trust someone code-named Curveball.

The Iraq invasion and the policy of preventive war favored by conservatives—and too many Democrats—after 9/11 are now recognized as the disasters they were. And that's just one of many mistakes that liberals work to address. Trickle-down economics, still being pushed by the Right, should take its rightful place in the trash bin of history, as the rich keep getting richer under the Reagan–Bush economic policies we've yet to shed. It was laughable that conservatives kept saying we needed low tax rates to create jobs and then complained about the lack of job creation while the low tax rates they initiated during the Bush 43 administration were still in effect.

The trope pushed by the Right that there's no such thing as global warming and that it certainly can't be because we're mucking up the planet has been discredited by scientific evidence presented earlier in these pages. Even among those who now begrudgingly accept that climate change exists, a large contingent can't admit we help cause it. This brings to mind the great line by Chico Marx in the film *Duck Soup*: "Who are you going to believe, me or your own eyes?"

I believe we are in a struggle over whether or not we are going to save America. *~Newt Gingrich*

When Newt Gingrich made the above comment to the Conservative Political Action Conference in 2010, I hardly think his intention was to help make the point that the saving would be at the hands of liberals. But thanks, Mr. Speaker, for the quote, for it's true. If we had listened to regressives all along, we'd never have achieved workers' rights or civil rights. Women wouldn't have the vote. The military would still be firing needed personnel because of sexual preference. Same-sex couples would not be allowed legally to love who they love. And women would still be getting back-alley abortions or bleeding to death while attempting to self-abort. America has indeed come a very long way (and you've come a very long way in this book, so thank you), but there is much yet to accomplish.

Lest we think we can rest on our liberal laurels because these battles are already won, think again. Workers in Ohio, Michigan, and Wisconsin are fighting to retain rights that unions have gained over the years. Wisconsin Governor Scott Walker, even as he was facing a recall, waited until the end of Good Friday 2012 to release a list of 51 laws he signed in two days. It was as if, while we were looking the other way, someone slipped a Mickey in our collective drink. Three of these sneakily created laws are particularly odious: one of them bans abortion coverage from insurance policies obtained through the state health-insurance exchange. More insulting to women is the requirement that any woman seeking an abortion must have a one-on-one consultation with a doctor, with no one else present, to determine if she is being pressured to make one choice over the other. Hey, it's not as if the little lady can think for herself, right? And any doctor who doesn't comply can be charged with a felony. To further insult and alienate women, Walker repealed the 2009 Equal Pay Enforcement Act that allowed victims of wage discrimination to plead their cases in state court rather than in the more-expensive federal system, practically insuring the continuation of unfair labor practices. In Arizona, Governor Jan Brewer signed a law in April 2012 to ban abortions after 20 weeks, except in rare emergency cases. Of course, the real goal, in all these cases, is to travel that slippery slope until these hard-won rights disappear entirely.

Women, who make 77 cents for every dollar earned by a man, still have a way to go to get equal pay for equal work. They continue to assert their claim for reproductive choice in spite of the years-long efforts by conservatives to take that right away, which clearly is not abating. Democrats continue to fight voter suppression in Florida, Tennessee, Louisiana, and a handful of other states.

Gays are working for marriage equality where it doesn't already exist.

And astonishingly, conservatives—that group that most professes its love of the Constitution—keeps proposing ways to change it. They've tried for a balanced-budget amendment, one to establish school prayer, and another to protect the word "God" in the Pledge of Allegiance. Georgia's Democrat-in-name-only, Zell Miller, tried to overturn the Seventeenth Amendment with one that would have reverted us back to having senators appointed by state legislatures, taking power away from voters. The Federal Marriage Amendment has been proposed four times. It would define marriage as between a man and a woman and stop the states from allowing same-sex marriage. And yet I thought these conservatives were the ones who believed in states' rights. Louisiana Senator David Vitter wanted an anti-immigration amendment that would deny citizenship to anyone born in the United States unless one parent was a citizen, a permanent resident, or a member of the armed forces.

Luckily, to change the Constitution it takes two-thirds of Congress to propose an amendment and three-quarters of state legislatures to ratify it. These are purposely high bars, but that hasn't stopped the Right from tilting at windmills, with proposed amendments like one to make flag-burning illegal and others to overturn *Roe v. Wade*. In fact, there have been 330 proposals to undo that decision, all of which failed. Conservatives keep trying but, thankfully, these efforts don't go anywhere. It's a good thing most of the country doesn't agree with them.

Besides trying to amend the Constitution, there is a movement among conservatives to declare that parts of the document they don't agree with are invalid. In particular, the Sixteenth Amendment, ratified in 1913, really bothers many on the Right, as it gives the federal government the right to collect an income tax. Conservatives have tried for years to prove this unconstitutional, claiming it was never properly ratified. They've used bizarre arguments like the claim that the word *income* could not be applied to wages or that wages could not be considered income because labor is bartered for them. Another protest was based on the theory that taxing income violates an individual's right to personal property. One contingent of objectors to the Sixteenth Amendment believes that the necessary number of states didn't ratify it because Ohio wasn't a state at the time. That must have been a huge surprise to Ohioans, who achieved statehood in 1803. Notable court cases challenging this amendment came from those trying to avoid paying taxes. Of course, that is the real goal of the Sixteenth Amendment deniers—to somehow get out of their dutiful obligation to pay income taxes.

From this conservative wish list of amendments they'd like to see either added or subtracted, it appears as though liberals are the ones protecting the Constitution. If saving America means preserving the vision of our founders, it's liberals to the rescue, and the need for rescue is acute when there are barbarians at the gate.

I want to put a ding in the universe. *~Steve Jobs*

We strive to be number one on so many of the issues we've discussed here, and we are—but not always where it counts. We're number one in military spending. Indeed, we're way beyond number one, spending more than the next 25 countries combined. We're 17th in childhood poverty, according to UNICEF, with 21.9 percent of children living below the poverty line. In Gross Domestic Product per capita, we come in 11th, and we're 38th in literacy, according to the Mundi Index. In income inequality, we rank 32nd out of 39 countries measured by the U.N.

If we are truly to live up to our promise as the world's greatest nation, the beacon of light for the rest of the world, the land that will "put a ding in the universe," how can we rest until no American has to fear the lack of basic human needs? No American should ever have to worry about a hot meal or a warm place to sleep. Mitt Romney's "I'm not concerned about the very poor—we have a safety net there" totally ignores what should be our goal, which is to do as much as possible to eliminate poverty, not to remain content that we can prop it up. Just compare Romney's rhetoric with the very real actions of Lyndon Johnson, for example, and you can see the difference in priorities between the Left and the Right. But the very poor are not where the voting base is, certainly not the Republican voting base pandered to by Mitt Romney.

Imagine how much better our health-care numbers would be if we made such a basic need available to all Americans, just as Medicare serves older folks. The United States is ranked 37th out of 191 countries by the World Health Organization, using performance indicators such as the overall health of the population, inequality of health within the population, patient satisfaction, and how the financial burden of health care is distributed within the population. The Commonwealth Fund has us last on its list of six industrialized nations, using markers like efficiency, cost, equity, and lifespan. Were it not for Republicans and conservative-to-moderate Blue Dog Democrats, we could at least have had a public option by now, so that private insurance companies would have more competition. We could have also implemented the simple Medicare for All Act from Congressman Conyers.

And we certainly have a way to go before we truly live up to Martin Luther King, Jr.'s, standard that we judge each other not by the color of our skin but by the content of our character. We have seen the difficulty some of our countrymen have had with our first black president. African Americans, along with other groups, are still working toward being regarded equally in our society. Mexicans, for example, are treated differently from other immigrants. Under the "wet foot, dry foot" policy, a Cuban who risks his or her life traveling the high seas and makes it to land in the United States has a pathway to residency. A Mexican who has a similar struggle but comes via the desert rather than the ocean is told his dry feet are no good here. Muslims are regarded in America the way Jews and Catholics once were (and, in some quarters, are still).

But don't despair! With history as our guide, we can have great hope for our future. America has come this far not only because of the brave men and women who have sacrificed their lives on battlefields, but also because of those who've dedicated their lives to improving the plight of everyday Americans. The domestic battles we've waged are every bit as important as the foreign ones. Over time, not only do progressives win the day, but all Americans, liberal or not, come to appreciate what has been won, even as they forget that their conservative predecessors opposed those advances when they were first proposed.

As we become a more diverse nation, the influx of new voters will likely lean Democratic, and this will help preserve the advances we have achieved. This is a major reason Republicans have been fighting to narrow voting rights, as they know a changing America will leave them trampled by the march of history. They are losing their grip, clinging to a dying past. The Census Bureau estimates that by 2020, minorities under age 18 will actually be in the majority, and this will apply to the general population by 2040. Non-Hispanic whites, the core of the Republican Party, are rapidly diminishing in numbers and now represent the minority of births in the United States.

The rallying cry of the Tea Party when it started was that they wanted to "take our country back." This came against the backdrop of, as Frank Rich put it, "a black president and a female speaker of the House—topped off by a wise Latina on the Supreme Court and a powerful gay Congressional committee chairman . . . sow[ing] fears of disenfranchisement among a dwindling and threatened minority." Sorry, Charlie, but you can't take a country back to an era that no longer exists. To borrow and slightly alter the title of that great Scorsese movie, America doesn't live there anymore. Besides, the only people who have the right to "take our country back" are Native Americans. The late Native American theologian and historian Vine Deloria, Jr., remarked, "When asked by an anthropologist what the Indians called America before the white man came, an Indian said simply, 'Ours.'"

I've spoken of the shining city all my political life, but I don't know if I ever quite communicated what I saw when I said it. But in my mind, it was a tall, proud city built on rocks stronger than oceans, windswept, God-blessed, and teeming with people of all kinds living in harmony and peace . . . And if there had to be city walls, the walls had doors and the doors were open to anyone with the will and the heart to get here. That's how I saw it, and see it still. ~*Ronald Reagan*

So what do I see as the future of America? Well, (as Reagan, the Great Communicator, would say to preface many pronouncements) I may not have agreed with many of his prescriptions, but I share and even admire his optimistic, sunny prognosis. History is not going to reverse itself. Workers won't lose rights, even as they must fight to retain them. Even if they do lose the occasional battle, as has happened in Wisconsin, they'll still win in the long run, as workers realize their best interests are served by progressives. Labor has one major thing going for it: safety in numbers. After all, there are more of us than there are of them. We will more and more realize the great contributions workers, documented or not, make to our culture and well-being.

Government will come to be recognized as an instrument of good. Tax rates will be adjusted as economic necessities require. Environmental changes will dictate better policy. We'll see drug addiction as an illness, not a crime, as we do alcohol addiction, and we'll eventually stop locking people up who choose to engage in the moderate use of drugs. Dumb laws that prevent pain sufferers from getting medical marijuana will disappear, as will drug laws that cost us too much money and infringe on our personal freedoms.

I truly believe these things will happen, and that it is still—to use another great phrase from the Gipper—morning in America. Our day is just beginning. It will be a day where women make as much money as men for the same work and no longer have to worry about their reproductive choices being taken away; where gays can marry, raise children, and go about their business with no concern that they will be stigmatized or hurt in any way. Same-sex couples, who can already get married in some states, will have their marriages recognized nationally. As gays gain more equality, those opposed will realize that their own marriages aren't in jeopardy because same-gender folks can be legally united. Gays can serve openly in the military now, and in time, even those opposed to that idea will accept it, just as regressives came to accept serving with blacks.

The day will come when African Americans will be elected to the highest offices without suspicion that their worldviews lack Americanism. Workers will not have to feel threatened by bosses and bureaucracies that would take away their right to bargain for their livelihood and their dignity. Every American will have enough food to eat, enough heating oil, and access to health care, regardless of income level. Immigrants, the elderly, the poor, the young, minorities, the infirm—"the least among us" as Jesus put it—will no longer fear that their voting rights, or any other rights for that matter, will be taken away.

This is the America I believe in. This is the America liberals have worked toward and will continue to create. Over time, Americans will come to see how the tremendous progress liberals achieved during our short existence benefits us all. Even though we stand at America's dawn, we can see the arc of the day. Because of all that we have done, because of all that we are, and because of all that we dream to be, we can thank the liberals for saving America. And by liberals, I mean all of us.

NOTES

Introduction

"the 'Washington takeover' of healthcare": The Language of Healthcare 2009, Frank Luntz, http://wonkroom.thinkprogress .org/wp-content/uploads/2009/05/frank-luntz-the-language-of-healthcare-20091.pdf?mobile=nc.

Chapter One: You're A Liberal (But May Not Know It)

Constitution: http://constitutionus.com/.

Declaration of Independence: http://www.archives.gov/exhibits/charters/declaration_transcript.html.

"We went to the company . . . ": Emily Friedman, "Romney Explains Record of Hiring Illegal Immigrants as Lawn Keepers," ABC News Blog (October 18, 2011): http://abcnews.go.com/blogs/politics/2011/10/romney-explains-record-of-hiring-illegal-immigrants-as-lawn-keepers/.

"Well, it is a hypothetical situation . . . ": Kevin Sack, "Quayle Insists Abortion Remarks Don't Signal Change in His View," *The New York Times* (July 24, 1992): http://www.nytimes .com/1992/07/24/us/quayle-insists-abortion-remarks-don't -signal-change-in-his-view.html?pagewanted=all&src=pm.

"I think it would be a positive thing . . . ": "Mitt Romney Says Stop Talking to Democrats—Mitt Romney Should Stop Being a Democrat," American Presidency Project (March 1, 2012): http://www.presidency.ucsb.edu/ws/index .php?pid=99795#ixzz1tXFMi3ZA.

"So when asked, 'Will I preserve . . . ": Alexander Burns, "Santorum Super PAC Robos Against 'Romneycare,'" Politico (February 28, 2012): http://www.politico.com/blogs /burns-haberman/2012/02/santorum-super-pac-robos-against -romneycare-115833.html.

"It hit me very hard . . . ": Steve Benen, "On the Anniversary of Roe v. Wade," Political Animal Blog, Washington Monthly, (January 23, 2012): http://www.washingtonmonthly.com /political-animal/2012_01/on_the_anniversary_of_roe_v _wa034920.php.

"state funding of abortion services . . . ": Jennifer Rubin, "Mitt Romney's Conversion," *The Weekly Standard* 12, no. 20 (February 5, 2007): http://www.weeklystandard.com/Content/Public /Articles/000/000/013/222htyos.asp.

"help kill black babies . . . ": Fred Lucas, "Herman Cain: It's Not Planned Parenthood—No, It's Planned Genocide," CNSnews .com (March 15, 2011): http://cnsnews.com/news/article /herman-cain-it-s-not-planned-parenthood-no-it-s-planned -genocide.

Morgan/Cain interview: "Interview with Herman Cain," *Piers Morgan Tonight* (October 19, 2011): http://transcripts.cnn.com /TRANSCRIPTS/1110/19/pmt.01.html.

"The problem is they are trying . . . ": Peter Nicholas, "White House Stirs Gay Marriage Debate," STLtoday.com (December 25, 2010): http://www.stltoday.com/news/national /article_7e84b441-3d42-52e0-8653-5ad109f70870.html.

"Well, I don't try to run my children's lives . . . ": Andrea Sachs, "Phyllis Schlafly at 84," *Time* (April 7, 2009): http://www.time .com/time/nation/article/0,8599,1889757,00.html.

"You're my daughter and I love you . . . ": Mary Cheney, *Now It's My Turn* (Threshold Editions, New York: 2006): 34.

"Segregation today . . . ": The 1963 Inaugural Address of Governor George C. Wallace (January 14, 1963): http://www
.archives.alabama.gov/govs_list/inauguralspeech.html.

"I have learned what suffering means . . . ": Lloyd Rohler, *George Wallace: Conservative Populist* (Praeger, Santa Barbara, CA: 2004): 85.

"a humanity so often lacking in his actions . . . ": Stephan Lesher, *George Wallace: American Populist* (Perseus Publising, Cambridge, MA: 1994): 501.

"except for the most confirmed standpatter . . . ": George McGovern, "The Case for Liberalism: A Defense of the Future Against the Past," *Harpers* (December 2002): 37–42.

Chapter Two: Have You Thanked A Liberal Today?

"Virtually every step forward . . . ": George McGovern, "The Case for Liberalism: A Defnse of the Future Against the Past," *Harpers* (December 2002): 37–42.

"only about 60 percent of the Obama plan . . . ": Paul Krugman, "The Obama Gap," *The New York Times,* Op. Ed. (January 8, 2009): http://www.nytimes.com/2009/01/09
/opinion/09krugman.html.

"un-American, illegal and infamous conspiracy": "A Short History of American Labor," Adapted from *AFL-CIO American Federationist* 88, no. 3 (March 1981): http://cdn.calisphere.org
/data/28722/2t/bk0003z4v2t/files/bk0003z4v2t-FID1.pdf.

"the elevation of the lowest paid worker . . . ": Stuart B. Kaufman, ed., *The Samuel Gompers Papers: The Making of a Union Leader, 1850–86, Volume 1* (University of Illinois Press, Champaign, IL: 1986): 73.

Williams/Gingrich questioning: Fox News Debate in Myrtle Beach, SC (January 16, 2012): http://www.youtube.com
/watch?v=4c1-22w2G7M.

"It's clear that the people have spoken": ABC 6 News, Columbus, OH: http://www.abc6onyourside.com/shared/newsroom /features/your_voice/videos/wsyx_vid_714.shtml.

"spent too much time at Harvard": Alex Seitz-Wald, "Romney, Who Has Two Harvard Degrees, Says Obama Spent 'Too Much Time At Harvard,'" *thinkprogress.org* (April 5, 2012): http:// thinkprogress.org/special/2012/04/05/458987/romney-who -has-two-harvard-degrees-says-obama-has-spent-too-much -time-at-harvard/?mobile=nc.

"higher education shall be made equally accessible . . . ": "International Covenant on Economic, Social and Cultural Rights," Office of the United Nation High Commissioner for Human Rights (1976): http://www2.ohchr.org/english/law/cescr.htm.

"We hold these truths to be self-evident . . . ": "Declaration of Sentiments Urged Equal Rights for Women," America.gov Archive (May 31, 2005): http://www.america.gov/st /pubsenglish/2005/May/20050531160341liameru oy0.2459375.html.

"I cannot respect the law as it exists today": "Sanger on Trial: The Brownsville Clinic Testimony" (Fall 2000): http://www .nyu.edu/projects/sanger/secure/newsletter/articles/sanger_on _trial.html.

"the right to copulate . . . ": Debora L. Spar and Briana Huntsberger, "The Business of Birth Contol," *Harvard Health Policy Review* 6, no. 1 (Spring 2005): 12: http://www.hcs.harvard.edu/~hhpr /publications/previous/05s/Spar_and_Huntsberger.pdf.

"undeniably feeble-minded . . . ": Charles Valenza, "Was Margaret Sanger a Racist?" *Family Planning Perspectives* 17, no. 1 (January–February 1985): 44–46.

"the Legislature may act to correct . . . ": Lilly M. Ledbetter v. The Good-Year Tire & Rubber Company, Inc., United States court of appeals for the eleventh circuit (May 29, 2007): http://caselaw .lp.findlaw.com/scripts/getcase.pl?court=US&vol=000&inv ol=05-1074.

"the amendment imposes a special disability . . . ": Romer v. Evans, Supreme Court of Colorado (May 20, 1996): http://caselaw.lp.findlaw.com/cgi-bin/getcase.pl?court=us&vol=000&invol=u10179.

"But freedom is not enough . . . ": Commencement Address at Howard University, "To Fulfill These Rights" (June 4, 1965): http://www.lbjlib.utexas.edu/johnson/archives.hom/speeches.hom/650604.asp.

"It threatens my marriage . . . ": Michael Sokolove, "The Believer," *The New York Times Magazine* (May 22, 2005): http://www.nytimes.com/2005/05/22/magazine/22SANTORUM.html?pagewanted=all.

"fulfills any definitional criteria . . . ": Miguel Braschi v. Stahl Associates Company, Court of Appeals of New York (July 6, 1989): http://www.iso.gmu.edu/~weitzman/braschiv.htm.

"weapons disturbance . . . ": Dale Carpenter, *Flagrant Conduct* (W. W. Norton & Co., Inc., New York: 2012).

"deviant sexual behavior . . . ": John Geddes Lawrence and Tyron Garner v. Texas, Court of Appeals of Texas, Fourteenth District (June 26, 2003): http://law2.umkc.edu/faculty/projects/ftrials/conlaw/lawrencevtexas.html.

"a tragic day for America . . . ": Robin Abcarian and Jessica Garrison, "Gains outweigh setbacks in a landmark year for gay rights," *Los Angeles Times* (December 19, 2010): http://articles.latimes.com/2010/dec/19/nation/la-na-gay-rights-year-20101219.

"In 2010, when I was deployed to Iraq . . . ": Z. Byron Wolf, "Debate Crowd Booed Gay Soldier," ABC News Blog (September 23, 2011): http://abcnews.go.com/blogs/politics/2011/09/debate-crowd-booed-gay-soldier/.

Chapter Three: Progress Affirmed!

"One thing, however, is certain . . . ": Bush v. Gore, the Florida
Supreme Court (December 12, 2000): http://www.law.cornell
.edu/supct/html/00-949.ZD.html. *"The availability and
use . . . ":* James Vicini, "Supreme Court limits police use of
GPS to track suspects," *Reuters* (January 23, 2012): http://
newsandinsight.thomsonreuters.com/Legal/News/2012/01
_-_January/Supreme_Court_limits_police_use_of_GPS_to
_track_suspects/.

"any drug, medicinal article or instrument . . . ": Griswold v.
Connecticut, Appeal from the Supreme Court of Errors of
Connecticut (June 7, 1965): http://www.law.cornell.edu
/supct/html/historics/USSC_CR_0381_0479_ZO.html.

"The most stringent protection of free speech . . . ": Alex McBride,
"Landmark Cases: Schenck v. U.S.," pbs.org: http://www.pbs
.org/wnet/supremecourt/capitalism/landmark_schenck.html.

"drunk off our God-fearing asses on Campari . . . ": Excerpt from
the Testimony of Larry Flynt (December 6, 19584): http://
law2.umkc.edu/faculty/projects/ftrials/falwell/flynttestimony
.html.

"may not, however, proscribe particular conduct . . . ": Texas v.
Johnson, U.S. Supreme Court (June 21, 1989): http://supreme
.justia.com/cases/federal/us/491/397/case.html.

Chapter Four: Liberal Values are American Values

"Who Pays?" Blitzer wanted to know . . . ": Sam Stein, "GOP
Tea Party Debate: Audience Cheers, Says Society Should Let
Uninsured Patient Die," *Huffington Post* (September 12, 2011):
http://www.huffingtonpost.com/2011/09/12/tea-party-debate
-health-care_n_959354.html.

"There is an important connection . . . ": "Transcript Highlights: The Medicaid Expansion Arguments," Kaiser Health News (March 28, 2012): http://www.kaiserhealthnews.org /stories/2012/march/28/medicaid-expansion-excerpts.aspx.

"The truth is that right after 9/11, I had a pin . . . ": "Obama Dropped Flag Pin in War Statement," ABC News: http:// abcnews.go.com/Politics/story?id=3690000&page=1# .T5Cs592Gq40.

"After a while, you start noticing people wearing a lapel pin . . . ": Jeff Zeleny "Obama's Lapels," *The New York Times* blog: The Caucus (October 4, 2007): http://thecaucus.blogs.nytimes .com/2007/10/04/obamas-lapels/.

"Maybe at Harvard law . . . ": Steve Gilbert, "Obama: Flag Pin Substitute for Patriotism," *Sweetness & Light* (October 4, 2007): http://sweetness-light.com/archive/barack-obama-wont-wear -american-flag-pin.

"I believe in an America . . . ": Mark Steyn, "The Man Who Gave Us Newt," National Review Online (January 22, 2010): http://www.nationalreview.com/corner/288873/man-who -gave-us-newt-mark-steyn.

"We believe that the best of America . . . ": Juliet Eilperin, "Palin's 'Pro-America Areas" Remark: Extended Version," *The Washington Post's* The Trail (October 17, 2008): http:// voices.washingtonpost.com/44/2008/10/17/palin_clarifies _her_pro-americ.html.

"there's something I know . . . ": Tim Mak, "Nancy Pelosi: There's no Newt Gingrich secret," *Politico* (January 25, 2012): http:// www.politico.com/news/stories/0112/71941.html.

"lives in a San Francisco environment . . . ": Alicia Cohn, "Gingrich says Pelosi is living in a fantasy world," *The Hill* (January 25, 2012): http://thehill.com/video/ campaign/206429-gingrich-says-pelosi-is-living-in-a -fantasy-if-she-thinks-she-has-dirt-on-him.

"Baghdad by the Bay": "A Sort of Homecoming," sfist.com
(November 30, 2006): http://sfist.com/2006/11/30/a_sort_of
_homecoming.php.

"Incredibly, the U.S. is being ruled . . . ": Dinesh D'Souza,
"How Obama Thinks," *Forbes* magazine (September 27, 2010):
http://www.forbes.com/forbes/2010/0927/politics-socialism
-capitalism-private-enterprises-obama-business-problem.html.

"stunning insight . . . the most profound insight . . . ": Robert
Costa, "Gingrich: Obama's 'Kenyan, anti-colonial' world-
view," National Review Online (September 11, 2010): http://
www.nationalreview.com/corner/246302/gingrich-obama
-s-kenyan-anti-colonial-worldview-robert-costa.

"a European radical attitude . . . ": "Gingrich Blasts Obama in
VA Stop for Signatures," *The Associated Press* on Newsmax.com
(December 22, 2011): http://www.newsmax.com/Politics
/Gingrich-obama/2011/12/22/id/421879.

*"tangible things . . . books, records, papers, documents, and
other items . . . ":* Committee Reports, 112th Congress (2011–
2012), Senate Report 112-013, "The USA Patriot Act Sunset
Extension Act of 2011," http://thomas.loc.gov/cgi-bin
/cpquery/?&sid=cp112InZRb&r_n=sr013.112&dbname
=cp112&&sel=TOC_276920&.

"Inconsistencies of opinion . . . " Daniel Webster,
The Works of Daniel Webster, Volume V (Little, Brown
and Company, Boston: 1857): 187: http://archive.org
/stream/worksofdanielweb030652mbp#page/n201/mode
/2up/search/The+Tariff.

"The essence of the Liberal outlook . . . ": Bertrand Russell,
Bertrand Russell Bundle: Unpopular Essays (Routledge,
New York: 2009): 15.

"reality-based community . . . ": Ron Suskind, "Without a
Doubt," *The New York Times Magazine* reposted at ronsuskind
.com (October 17, 2004): http://www.ronsuskind.com/
articles/000106.html.

"Mr. Obama told the French . . . ": Karl Rove, "The President's Apology Tour," *The Wall Street Journal* online (April 23, 2009): http://online.wsj.com/article/SB124044156269345357.html.

"But in Europe, there is an anti-Americanism . . . ": "Remarks by President Obama at Strasbourg Town Hall" (April 3, 2009): http://www.whitehouse.gov/the_press_office/Remarks-by -President-Obama-at-Strasbourg-Town-Hall.

"This agency forbade . . . ": "Remarks of Kevin Gover, Assistant Secretary-Indian Affairs: Address to Tribal Leaders," *Journal of American Indian Education* 39, no. 2 (Winter 2000): http://jaie .asu.edu/v39/V39I2A1.pdf.

"The United States Government did something that was wrong . . . ": "An Apology 65 Years Late" *PBS NewsHour* with Jim Lehrer (April 16, 1997): http://www.pbs.org/newshour/bb/health /jan-june97/tuskegee_5-16.html.

"We have seen more than once . . . ": Buck v. Bell, Error to the Supreme Court of Appeals of the State of Virginia (May 2, 1927): http://www.law.cornell.edu/supct/html/historics /USSC_CR_0274_0200_ZO.html.

"On behalf of the state . . . ": Kevin Begos, Danielle Deaver, and John Railey, "Easley Apologizes to Sterilization Victims," JournalNow.com (December 13, 2002): http://extras .journalnow.com/againsttheirwill/parts/epilogue/story4.html.

"I want this solved on my watch . . . ": Michelle Kessel and Jessica Hopper "Victims Speak Out About North Carolina Sterilization Program, Which Targeted Women, Young Girls and Blacks," *Rock Center with Brian Williams* (November 7, 2011): http://rockcenter.msnbc.msn.com/_news/2011/11/07 /8640744-victims-speak-out-about-north-carolina -sterilization-program-which-targeted-women-young -girls-and-blacks.

"To be a liberal, according to my favorite scripture . . . ": Rev. Kimi Riegel, "What is Liberal Religion" (December 2005): http://www.northwestuu.org/old_site/sermons_05_06 /sermonLiberalreligion.html.

Chapter Five: Who's Your Deity?

"I believe in an America where the separation of church and state . . . ": John F. Kennedy, "Address to Protestant Ministers" (September 12, 1960): http://www.npr.org/templates/story /story.php?storyId=16920600.

"The idea that the church can have no influence . . . ": Alana Horowitz, "Santorum: Separation of Church and State 'Makes Me Want to Throw Up,'" *The Huffington Post* (February 26, 2012): http://www.huffingtonpost.com/2012/02/26 /santorum-church-and-state_n_1302246.html.

"the criterion by which the Bible is to be interpreted is Jesus Christ": Bob Allen, "Jimmy Carter Discusses Bible," Associated Baptist Press (March 27, 2012): http://www.abpnews.com /content/view/7261/53/.

"In addition to all the weaknesses . . . ": Mario Cuomo, "Religious Belief and Public Morality: A Catholic Governor's Perspective" (September 13, 1984): http://archives.nd.edu /research/texts/cuomo.htm?DocID=14

"Democracy demands that the religiously motivated . . . " Barack Obama, "The Connection Between Faith and Politics" (June 28, 2006): http://www.realclearpolitics.com/articles/2006/06 /the_connection_between_faith_p.html.

"some phony theology . . . ": Jan Crawford, "Santorum Remark on Obama 'Theology' Draws Ire" (February 20, 2012): http://www.cbsnews.com/8301-505267_162-57381228 /santorum-remark-on-obama-theology-draws-ire/.

"One of the things I will talk about . . . ": Michael Scherer, "Rick Santorum Wants to Fight 'the Dangers of Contraception,'" *Time* magazine online, Swampland (February 14, 2012): http://swampland.time.com/2012/02/14/rick-santorum -wants-to-fight-the-dangers-of-contraception/#ixzz1mSfcFx5l.

"not appropriate or qualified . . . ": Laura Bassett and Amanda Terkel, "House Democrats Walk Out Of One-Sided Hearing On Contraception, Calling It An 'Autocratic Regime,'" *The Huffington Post* (February 16, 2012): http://www.huffingtonpost .com/2012/02/16/contraception-hearing-house-democrats -walk-out_n_1281730.html.

"If I wanted the government in my womb . . . ": Laura Bassett, "Oklahoma Personhood Bill Ignites Feminist Movement," *The Huffington Post* (February 29, 2012): http://www .huffingtonpost.com/2012/02/29/oklahoma-personhood -fetal-personhood-bill_n_1310992.htm.

"We should show the same attention . . . ": Laura Bassett, "Nina Turner, Ohio State Senator, Introduces Viagra Bill To Counter Anti-Contraception Legislation," *The Huffington Post* (March 13, 2012): http://www.huffingtonpost.com/2012/03 /13/nina-turner-viagra-contraception-bills_n_1341642.html.

"spilled semen amendment": Constance Johnson, "About My 'Spilled Semen' Amendment to Oklahoma's Personhood Bill," *The Guardian* (February 9, 2012): http://www.guardian.co.uk /commentisfree/cifamerica/2012/feb/09/spilled-semen -amendment-oklahoma-personhood-bill.

"each 'egg person' and each 'sperm person' . . . ": Resolution 3641, Wilmington, DE (March 1, 2012): http://www .wilmingtonde.gov/docs/1029/3641.pdf.

"It sounds like they're mocking prolife-bills." Laura Bassett, "Nina Turner, Ohio State Senator, Introduces Viagra Bill To Counter Anti-Contraception Legislation," *The Huffington Post* (March 13, 2012): http://www.huffingtonpost.com/2012/03/13/nina -turner-viagra-contraception-bills_n_1341642.html.

"rakers . . . mosque crawlers . . . ": "'Mosque Crawlers,' 'Rakers' Monitoring U.S. Muslims for NYPD," PBS NewsHour with Jim Lehrer (February 28, 2012): http://www.pbs.org/newshour/bb /law/jan-june12/nypd_02-28.html.

"to protect everyone . . . ": Alan Colmes, "New York Police Commissioner Defends Surveillance On Muslims," Fox News Radio: http://radio.foxnews.com/2012/02/28/new-york-police-commissioner-defends-surveillance-on-muslims/.

"creeping attempt . . . to gradually ease Sharia law and the Muslim faith into our government": Scott Keyes, "Herman Cain Tells ThinkProgress 'I Will Not' Appoint A Muslim In My Administration," *Think Progress* (March 26, 2011): http://"thinkprogress.org/politics/2011/03/26/153625/herman-cain-muslims/.

"That's not discrimination . . . ": Ashley Killough, "Herman Cain: Muslims Must Show Loyalty to Work for Me," CNN Political Ticker (June 10, 2011): http://politicalticker.blogs.cnn.com/2011/06/10/herman-cain-muslims-must-show-loyalty-to-work-for-me/.

"taking faith and crushing it . . . ": Michael Allen, "Rick Santorum Says Obama Leading Religious People to Guillotine," Opposing Views (February 9, 2012): http://www.opposingviews.com/i/religion/christianity/catholicism/video-rick-santorum-says-obama-leading-religious-people.

"the Obama administration's attack on Christianity . . . " Newt Gingrich, speech in Florida (January 30, 2012): http://www.nbcuniversalarchives.com/nbcuni/clip/51A8292_s01.do.

"fought against religion . . . ": "Romney: Obama has 'fought against religion,'" CBS News (February 22, 2012): http://www.cbsnews.com/8301-250_162-57382442/romney-obama-has-fought-against-religion.

"America is experiencing an Islamist cultural-political offensive . . . ": Paul Bedard, "Gingrich Blasts Plan for Mosque at Ground Zero," *U.S. News and World Report* online (July 23, 2010): http://www.usnews.com/news/washington-whispers/articles/2010/07/23/gingrich-blasts-plan-for-mosque-at-ground-zero.

"the potential for extremists . . . ": Nate Gunderson, "Romney Statement on the Ground Zero Mosque," Mitt Romney Central (August 10, 2010): http://mittromneycentral.com/2010/08/10/romney-statement-on-the-ground-zero-mosque/.

"where the earliest settlers first set foot in New Amsterdam . . . ": Michael Bloomberg, "Mayor Bloomberg Discusses the Landmarks Preservation Commission Vote on 45-47 Park Place" (August 3, 2010): www.nyc.gov/html/om/html/2010b/pr337-10.html.

"What did you have? A tuna sandwich? . . . ": Robert Klein, *The Amorous Busboy of Decatur Avenue* (Touchstone, New York: 2006): 10.

"build triumphal mosques . . . ": Tanya Somanader, "Pam Geller: Park51 Is 'The Second Wave Of The 9/11 Attack'" (November 24, 2010): http://thinkprogress.org/politics/2010/11/24/131936/pam-geller-park51.

"kick in the head . . . ": "A Mosque Near Ground Zero," CNN (June 6, 2010): http://www.youtube.com/watch?v=D_wqt9edqOQ&feature=related.

"the second wave of the 9/11 attacks . . . ": Tanya Somanader, "Pam Geller: Park51 Is 'The Second Wave Of The 9/11 Attack'" (November 24, 2010): http://thinkprogress.org/politics/2010/11/24/131936/pam-geller-park51.

"I love these Marines . . . ": Pamela Geller, "CAIR Condemns Alleged 'Desecration' of Dead Jihadists by U.S. Marines in Afghanistan," Atlas Shrugs (January 11, 2012): http://atlasshrugs2000.typepad.com/atlas_shrugs/2012/01/cair-condemns-alleged-desecration-of-dead-jihadists-by-us-marines-in-afghanistan.html.

"He has a ZERO rating from the American Conservative Union . . . ": Amy Gardner, "Tea Party's Judson Phillips Defends Essay Attacking Congressman for Being Muslim," *The Washington Post* online (October 28, 2010): http://www.washingtonpost.com/wp-dyn/content/article/2010/10/27/AR2010102705118.html.

"We demand that he does so immediately . . . ": Andy Birkey, "Anti-Muslim Group Calls for Ellison's Removal from Committee," *The Minnesota Independent* (October 7, 2010): http://minnesotaindependent.com/71967/anti-muslim -group-calls-for-ellisons-removal-from-committee.

"Mr. Hamdani bravely sacrificed his life . . . ": Zaid Jilani, "Rep. Ellison Breaks Into Tears Explaining Story Of Muslim First Responder Who Died To Save Americans On 9/11," Think Progress (March 10, 2011): http://thinkprogress.org/politics /2011/03/10/149775/ellison-tears-king-hearing/.

"too many mosques in this country . . . ": Daniel Reilly, "Rep. Peter King: There are "too many mosques in this country," Politico (September 19, 2007): http://www.politico.com/blogs /thecrypt/0907/Rep_King_There_are_too_many_mosques_in _this_country__Page3.html.

"Since 9/11, 77 extremist efforts . . . ": Jackie Speier, "Practicing Guilt by Association," *The Hill* (March 11, 2011): http:// thehill.com/blogs/congress-blog/homeland-security/148911 -practicing-guilt-by-association.

"This is not a Muslim problem . . . ": David Dayen, "Sheriff Lee Baca, Only Law Enforcement Witness at King's Muslim Radicalization Hearings, Speaks Out," Fire Dog Lake (March 9, 2011): http://news.firedoglake.com/2011/03/09/sheriff-lee-baca-only -law-enforcement-witness-at-kings-muslim-radicalization -hearings-speaks-out/.

"We all want progress . . . ": C.S. Lewis, *Mere Christianity* (Harper-Collins, New York: 2001): 28.

Chapter Six: America Has Issues

"Corporations are people, my friend . . . ": Philip Rucker, "Mitt Romney Says 'Corporations Are People' at Iowa State Fair," *The Washington Post* (August 11, 2011): http://www .washingtonpost.com/politics/mitt-romney-says-corporations-are-people/2011/08/11/gIQABwZ38I_story.html.

"any Act of Congress . . . ": "Words Denoting Number, Gender, and So Forth," Cornell University Law School, Legal Information Institute: http://www.law.cornell.edu/uscode/text/1/1.

"Corporations Are Not People Act . . . ": "California Attorney General's Initiative Measures Title & Summary," Occupy Palos Verdes (March 15, 2012): http://occupypv.comule.com /articles.php?article_id=80.

"the food stamp president . . . ": Michael Allen, "Newt Gingrich Calls Obama the 'Food Stamp President,'" Opposing Views (January 17, 2012): http://www.opposingviews.com /i/politics/2012-election/video-newt-gingrich-calls-obama -food-stamp-president.

"Now many of our Christians . . . ": Paul Weyrich (1980): http://www.youtube.com/watch?v=8GBAsFwPglw.

"If they found a single case of a conspiracy . . .": Eric Lipton and Ian Urbina, "In 5 Year Effort, Scant Evidence of Voter Fraud," *New York Times* (April 12, 2007): http:// www.nytimes.com/2007/04/12/washington/12fraud. html?pagewanted=print.

"An unconstitutional law is void ab initio . . .": Andrew Harris, *Bloomberg* (March 20, 2012): http://www.bloomberg.com /news/2012-03-20/wisconsin-judge-won-t-stay-ruling-to -invalidate-voter-id-law-1-.html.

"In sum, however analyzed . . . ": Letter from the office of the Attorney General, U.S. Department of Justice (December 23, 2011): http://www.justice.gov/crt/about/vot/sec_5/ ltr/l_122311.php.

"If you want to reduce illegal immigration . . . ": Jason Riley, *The Colbert Report* (July 15, 2008): http://www.colbertnation.com /the-colbert-report-videos/176184/july-15-2008/jason-riley.

"to ensure that individuals being held by state . . . ": "ICE Establishes Hotline for Detained Individuals, Issues New Detainer Form," Press Release from U.S. Immigration and Customs

Enforcement (December 29, 2011): http://www.ice.gov/news/
releases/1112/111229washingtondc.htm.

"So when a family gets into a car . . . ": Edwin Mora, "Rep. Gri-
jalva: Arizona Immigration Law Profiles People Just As Tray-
von Martin Was Profiled," CNSNews.com (March 27, 2012):
http://cnsnews.com/news/article/rep-grijalva-arizona-
immigration-law-profiles-people-just-trayvon-martin-was-
profiled.

"The states have decisions to make . . . ": Elise Foley, "State AGs,
Democrats File Briefs Against Arizona Immigration Law," *The
Huffington Post* (March 27, 2012): http://www.huffingtonpost
.com/2012/03/27/arizona-immigration-law_n_1383923.html.

"The crime rate in Arizona in 2008 . . . ": Daniel Griswold,
"Misguided Fears of Crime Fuel Arizona Immigration Law,"
Cato @ Liberty, Cato Institute (April 27, 2010): http://www
.cato-at-liberty.org/misguided-fears-of-crime-fuel-arizona
-immigration-law/.

"Removing low-skilled immigrant workers . . . ": Daniel Griswold,
"Illegal Immigrant Crackdown Would Backfire on Pa.," *Patriot
News* (September 18, 2011): http://www.pennlive.com/
editorials/index.ssf/2011/09/illegal_immigrant_crackdown_wo
.html.

Cato Report on drugs: Jeffrey A. Miron and Katherine Waldock,
White Paper "The Budgetary Impact of Ending Drug Prohibition," Cato Institute (September 27, 2010): http://www.cato
.org/publications/white-paper/budgetary-impact-ending-drug
-prohibition.

"has disastrous implications for national security . . . ": Jeffrey
Miron, "Commentary: Legalize Drugs to Stop Violence," *CNN*
(March 24, 2009): http://edition.cnn.com/2009/
POLITICS/03/24/miron.legalization.drugs/.

"if it's all about equality . . . ": "Santorum: Gay Marriage Is Like Incest" (February 22, 2012): http://www.alan.com/?s=santoru m+michelangelo+signorile+2008+gay+marriage+incest.

"Unless we protect (the family) . . . ": "Rick Santorum: Gay Marriage Would Make Our Country Fall," *The Huffington Post* (November 21, 2011): http://www.huffingtonpost .com/2011/11/21/rick-santorum-gay-marriag_n_1105063 .html.

"Here is 1 effect . . . ": "Santorum Tweets: 'Here is One Effect of Changing (the) Definition of Marriage,'" National Organization of Marriage (December 19, 2011): http://www.nomblog .com/16919/?doing_wp_cron.

"not consistent with the Constitution . . . ": "Rick Santorum One-on-One with Chuck Todd," *NBC Nightly News* (December 30, 2011): http://video.msnbc.msn.com/nightly-news/ 45829898/#45829898.

"be a hit to faith and family in America . . . ": Shushannah Walshe, "Rick Santorum Has Tense Exchange on Gay Rights and Health Care in Iowa," *ABC News* (December 6, 2011): http://abcnews.go.com/blogs/politics/2011/12/rick-santorum-has-tense-exchange-on-gay-rights-and-health-care-in-iowa/.

"My mommy—Miss Bachmann—my mommy's gay . . . ": "Michele Bachmann Meets Young LGBT Activist Elijah At Book Signing, *The Huffington Post* (December 5, 2011): http:// www.huffingtonpost.com/2011/12/05/michele-bachmann -elijah-activist-_n_1130591.html.

"I believe marriage is between a man and a woman . . . ": "Mitt Romney: Court Decision on Proposition 8 'Does Not End This Fight,'" MittRomney.com (February 7, 2012): http://www .mittromney.com/news/press/2012/02/mitt-romney-court -decision-proposition-8-does-not-end-fight.

"At a personal level, I wish I had spoken out . . . ": Thomas Schaller, "Same Sex, Opposite Impact," Salon.com (March 2, 2012): http://www.salon.com/2012/03/02/same_sex _opposite_impact/.

"Endangered Republican Candidates Act . . . ": "The Defense of Marriage Act : Hearing Before the Committee on the Judiciary, United States Senate, One Hundred Fourth Congress" (July 11, 1996): http://www.archive.org/stream /defenseofmarriag00unit/defenseofmarriag00unit_djvu.txt.

"deny the protections, benefits, and obligations . . . ": "The Massachusetts Supreme Judicial Court Ruling on Homosexual Marriage" (November 18, 2003): http://www.massresistance.org /docs/marriage/sjcruling.html#top.

"only marriage between a man and a woman is valid . . . ": California Family Code 308-5: http://www.leginfo. ca.gov/cgi-bin/displaycode?section=fam&group=00001-01000&file=300-310.

"To be clear I believe . . . ": Jon Huntsman, Twitter (August 18, 2011): https://twitter.com/#!/jonhuntsman /statuses/104250677051654144.

"Science should get out of politics . . . ": William Petroski, "Santorum: Parents, Not Obama, Know What Is Best for Their Child's Education," *Des Moines Register* (December 9, 2011): http://caucuses.desmoinesregister.com/2011/12/09 /santorum-parents-not-obama-know-what-is-best-for-their -childs-education/.

Wall Street Journal op-ed: "No Need to Panic about Global Warming," *Wall Street Journal* (January 26, 2012): http:// online.wsj.com/article/SB10001424052970204301404577171 531838421366.html?mod=WSJ_Opinion_LEADTop.

Science magazine article: Jennifer Sills, ed., "Climate Change and the Integrity of Science," *Science* 328 (May 7, 2010): 689–691: http://www.sciencemag.org/content/328/5979/689 .full.pdf.

"this sector has remained rock-solid red . . . ": Campaign Contributions Related to Energy and Natural Gas, Open Secrets and the Center for Responsive Politics: http://www.opensecrets. org/industries/indus.php?Ind=E.

"I exhale carbon dioxide . . . ": Reid Epstein and Dan Berman, "Mitt Romney: 'I Exhale Carbon Dioxide," Politico (November 18, 2011): http://www.politico.com/news /stories/1111/68709.html#ixzz1eBpNiXEo.

"I have just completed Mike's Nature trick . . . ": "Beck's 'Brand New Reality' on Climate Change Relies on Distorting Apparently Stolen Emails," Media Matters (November 23, 2009): http://mediamatters.org/research/200911230052.

"To forestall or prevent . . . ": "Bush's National Security Strategy" (September 20, 2002): http://www.nytimes.com/2002/09/20 /politics/20STEXT_FULL.html?pagewanted=all.

"without preconditions . . . ": Anne Bayefsky, "A Talk-Is-Cheap Foreign Policy," *CBS News* (September 22. 2009): http://www .cbsnews.com/stories/2008/05/19/opinion/main4108435. shtml.

". . . if America is willing to come to the table . . . ": "The Obama-Biden Plan," Change.gov, the Office of the President Elect: http://change.gov/agenda/foreign_policy_agenda/.

"I would also point out that a Gingrich presidency . . . ": Ben Armbruster, "Gingrich: Iran 'Should Expect to Get Hit' If I'm President," Think Progress (March 2, 2012): http://thinkprogress .org/security/2012/03/02/436735/gingrich-iran-get-hit/.

"If Iran doesn't get rid of nuclear facilities . . . ": "Santorum at AIPAC: 'If Iran Doesn't Get Rid of Nuclear Facilities, We'll Tear Them Down Ourselves'": http://www.ricksantorum.com /news/2012/03/santorum-aipac-if-iran-doesnt-get-rid-nuclear -facilities-well-tear-them-down-ourselves

"I will make sure Iran knows . . . ": Emily Friedman, "Romney Accuses Obama of Dawdling with Iran Sanctions," *ABC News* (March 6, 2012): http://abcnews.go.com/blogs/politics /2012/03/romney-accuses-obama-of-dawdling-with-iran -sanctions/.

"If Barack Obama gets re-elected . . . ": Emily Friedman, "Iran Will Have Nukes If Obama Is Elected, Romney Says," *ABC News* (March 4, 2012): http://abcnews.go.com/blogs/politics /2012/03/iran-will-have-nukes-if-obama-is-re-elected -romney-says/.

"Either the ayatollahs will get the message . . . ": Mitt Romney, "How I Would Check Iran's Nuclear Ambition," *Washington Post* (March 5, 2012): http://www.washingtonpost.com /opinions/mitt-romney-how-i-would-check-irans-nuclear -ambition/2012/03/05/gIQAneYItR_story.html.

"Another term for preventive war . . . ": Ron Paul at Conservative Political Action Conference (CPAC) 2010: http://conservative .org/cpac/archives/cpacarchivescpac-2010-rep-ron-paul/.

"I strongly oppose House Joint Resolution 75 . . .": Ron Paul, "Statement in Opposition to House Resolution on Iraq" (December 19, 2001): http://paul.house.gov/index. php?option=com_content&task=view&id=370&Itemid=60.

"If at any time the intelligence community presents . . . ": Eli Clifton, "McConnell Threatens Congressional Resolution Authorizing Use of Force Against Iran," Think Progress (March 6, 2012): http://thinkprogress.org/security/2012/03/06/438444 /mcconnell-iran-war-resolution/.

"profound concerns . . . ": "Experts Commend North Korea Deal That Right-Wing Media are Attacking," Media Matters (March 8, 2012): http://mediamatters.org/research/201203080020.

Chapter Seven: You're Welcome!

"My main purpose . . . ": BBC Documentary *Modern Spies* Episode 2 (April 9, 2012): http://www.youtube.com /watch?v=lvKVGmAc54c.

"facts and conclusions based on solid intelligence . . . ": "Powell Presents US Case to Security Council of Iraq's Failure to Disarm," UN News Centre (February 5, 2003): http://www.un.org/ apps/news/storyAr.asp?NewsID=6079&Cr=iraq&Cr1=inspect.

"several mobile biological weapons labs . . . ": George W. Bush, "Address Before a Joint Session of the Congress on the State of the Union," The American Presidency Project (January 28, 2003): http://www.presidency.ucsb.edu/ws/index .php?pid=29645#axzz1sndDm19E.

"We went to war in Iraq on a lie . . . ": BBC Documentary *Modern Spies* Episode 2 (April 9, 2012): http://www.youtube.com /watch?v=lvKVGmAc54c.

"Who you gonna to believe . . . ": *Duck Soup* (1933): http://www .imdb.com/title/tt0023969/quotes.

"a black president and a female speaker of the House . . . ": Frank Rich, "The Rage Is Not About Health Care," *New York Times* (March 27, 2010): http://www.nytimes.com/2010/03/28 /opinion/28rich.html.

ACKNOWLEDGMENTS

As a longtime fan of Hay House and of Louise Hay, herself, it is extremely meaningful to me that they are the publishers of *Thank the Liberals*. I owe a special debt of gratitude to Dr. Wayne Dyer, whose friendship and whose Hay House books have given me so much sustenance. My thanks to Reid Tracy, who enabled this project, and to Patty Gift and Richelle Zizian for their dedication to this book. It would never have made it to its current form without my superb editor, Laura Koch, who sacrificed many long hours, weekends, and late nights. My longtime friend and personal manager, Rory Rosegarten, has been a guiding force in my career for more years than either of us wishes to admit. His creative contribution here, and in so many ways, is incalculable.

The visibility Fox News has given me has opened up worlds of opportunity for me, and for that I am most grateful to Roger Ailes, a remarkable news executive, leader, and friend. Bill Shine started at Fox as our show producer and it's no accident that he is now Executive Vice President of Programming. His advice and friendship have steered me in the right direction since our first day working together in 1996. My radio staff is the best in the business, and my gratitude goes to Senior Producer Joel Morton, my booker and assistant Robin Carson, studio producer Aimee De Benigno, engineer Josh Harmon, and production chief Rob Maurer. Mike Elder, Bob Finnerty, and Kevin Magee round out our executive team who, along with affiliate director Doug Murphy and his staff, Dave Manning and Jillian Schalk, see to it that our show is heard everywhere. My first radio agent, Adam Berg, is annoyed with me for not mentioning him in my last book. I told him I'd have to write another if only to correct that oversight. Okay, Adam, here ya go. Friends Sanford Teller and Andrew Napolitano offered wonderful input along the way in shaping this book and pals Michael Harrison and Paul Guercio are the world's best sounding boards. For support and encouragement a special nod goes to Patricia Greenwald.

I am blessed with a wonderful family. My sister, Susan, and her husband, Steve; my niece Ellen, her husband, David, and their children Lilith and Basha; and my nephews Mark and Gary. My mother-in-law, Pat, and sister-in-law Monica will continue to razz me about politics, especially after reading this book, but they are living proof that conservatives are generous and loving. There is no better application for the words "long-suffering" than to partners of those who write books. For that, I reserve special gratitude to my bride and soul mate, Jocelyn, to whom this book is dedicated.

ABOUT THE AUTHOR

Alan Colmes is a liberal political commentator, radio host, author, and web publisher. He currently hosts *The Alan Colmes Show*, a nationally syndicated radio show distributed by Fox News Radio. Offering a bold take on the news of the day, with guests ranging from prominent political figures to the biggest names in entertainment and pop culture, Colmes welcomes "any and all opinion, any and all of the time." Colmes runs the website Liberaland, where he covers the most recent and powerful stories in the news. He is also the author of the book *Red, White & Liberal*.

Colmes began his career in stand-up comedy but quickly moved into the world of broadcast news. After several highly rated radio shows, Colmes cemented his reputation as a liberal voice in the media when he served as the liberal counterpart to Sean Hannity on Fox News's *Hannity & Colmes*.

Website: **www.alan.com**

We hope you enjoyed this Hay House book. If you'd like to receive our online catalog featuring additional information on Hay House books and products, or if you'd like to find out more about the Hay Foundation, please contact:

Hay House, Inc., P.O. Box 5100, Carlsbad, CA 92018-5100
(760) 431-7695 or (800) 654-5126
(760) 431-6948 (fax) or (800) 650-5115 (fax)
www.hayhouse.com® • **www.hayfoundation.org**

* * *

Published and distributed in Australia by:
Hay House Australia Pty. Ltd., 18/36 Ralph St., Alexandria NSW 2015 •
Phone: 612-9669-4299 • *Fax:* 612-9669-4144 • www.hayhouse.com.au

Published and distributed in the United Kingdom by: Hay House UK, Ltd., 292B Kensal Rd., London W10 5BE • *Phone:* 44-20-8962-1230 • *Fax:* 44-20-8962-1239 • www.hayhouse.co.uk

Published and distributed in the Republic of South Africa by:
Hay House SA (Pty), Ltd., P.O. Box 990, Witkoppen 2068 •
Phone/Fax: 27-11-467-8904 • www.hayhouse.co.za

Published in India by: Hay House Publishers India, Muskaan Complex, Plot No. 3, B-2, Vasant Kunj, New Delhi 110 070 •
Phone: 91-11-4176-1620 • *Fax:* 91-11-4176-1630 • www.hayhouse.co.in

Distributed in Canada by: Raincoast, 9050 Shaughnessy St., Vancouver, B.C. V6P 6E5 • *Phone:* (604) 323-7100 •
Fax: (604) 323-2600 • www.raincoast.com

* * *

Take Your Soul on a Vacation

Visit **www.HealYourLife.com®** to regroup, recharge, and reconnect with your own magnificence. Featuring blogs, mind-body-spirit news, and life-changing wisdom from Louise Hay and friends.

Visit **www.HealYourLife.com** today!

Free Mind-Body-Spirit e-Newsletters

From Hay House, the Ultimate Resource for Inspiration

Be the first to know about Hay House's dollar deals, free downloads, special offers, affirmation cards, giveaways, contests, and more!

 Get exclusive excerpts from our latest releases and videos from *Hay House Present Moments*.

 Enjoy uplifting personal stories, how-to articles, and healing advice, along with videos and empowering quotes, within *Heal Your Life*.

 Have an inspirational story to tell and a passion for writing? Sharpen your writing skills with insider tips from *Your Writing Life*.

Receive uplifting affirmations, empowering thoughts, and healing wisdom from *Louise Hay*.

Discover ways to overcome all obstacles with the inspiring words of *Dr. Wayne Dyer* to get your wishes fulfilled.

Get angelic, heavenly assistance for your everyday life from angel expert and lifelong clairvoyant *Doreen Virtue*.

Uncover the timeless secrets of life from *Gregg Braden* and discover the collective wisdom of our past.

Get inspired, educate yourself, and share the wisdom!
Visit www.hayhouse.com to sign up today!

  HealYourLife.com ♥

Heal Your Life One Thought at a Time . . .
on Louise's All-New Website!

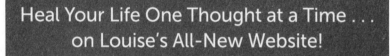

"Life is bringing me everything I need and more."

— Louise Hay

Come to HEALYOURLIFE.COM today and meet the world's best-selling self-help authors; the most popular leading intuitive, health, and success experts; up-and-coming inspirational writers; and new like-minded friends who will share their insights, experiences, personal stories, and wisdom so you can heal your life and the world around you . . . one thought at a time.

Here are just some of the things you'll get at HealYourLife.com:

- DAILY AFFIRMATIONS
- CAPTIVATING VIDEO CLIPS
- EXCLUSIVE BOOK REVIEWS
- AUTHOR BLOGS
- LIVE TWITTER AND FACEBOOK FEEDS
- BEHIND-THE-SCENES SCOOPS
- LIVE STREAMING RADIO
- "MY LIFE" COMMUNITY OF FRIENDS

PLUS:
FREE Monthly Contests and Polls
FREE BONUS gifts, discounts,
and newsletters

Make It Your Home Page Today!
www.HealYourLife.com®

HEAL YOUR LIFE®♥